TO BE A PERSON OF INTEGRITY

R. James Ogden, Editor

JUDSON PRESS, VALLEY FORGE

TO BE A PERSON OF INTEGRITY

Library of Congress Cataloging in Publication Data

Main entry under title:

To be a person of integrity.

    Includes bibliographical references.
    1. Bible—Biography. 2. Christian life—Baptist authors. 3. Bible—Study—Text-books. I. Ogden R. James.
BS605.2.T6   220.9'2 [B]   75-4901
ISBN 0-8170-0678-8

Printed in the U.S.A.

The photograph on page 11 is by John Goodwin, on pages 13 and 46 by Image, Inc., on pages 28 and 82 by Wallowitch, on page 37 by Steve Wall, on pages 60 and 68 by Harold Lambert, on page 73 by H. Armstrong Roberts, on page 84 by Vincent Franco, on page 89 by Bob Combs, on page 100 by John Stone, on page 108 by David Strickler, and on page 111 by Paul Alan.

Acknowledgments

This Bible study series was conceived during the meetings of an ad hoc group of American Baptists charged with preparing biblical resources for a three-year emphasis upon the development of an evangelistic life style. Participants in that group included Richard R. Broholm, Prentiss Pemberton, Phyllis Trible, Owen Owens, and myself. Phyllis Trible's insight that "all Scripture is a pilgrim, wandering through history, engaging in new settings, and ever refusing to be locked in the box of the past" was particularly formative ("Ancient Priests and Modern Pollutors," *Andover Newton Quarterly,* November, 1971). She continued to offer direct consultation during the development of the series.

Lenore Kruse has gone beyond the call of duty in using some of her retirement time to offer valuable editorial assistance, including the preparation of a manuscript on Peter to fill a last-minute gap. Owen Owens also graciously made a final contribution. Milton Ryder offered creative suggestions and consultation in the selection of photographs to accompany the text. The heaviest burdens of clerical work were carried by Pat Schell and Peggy Stewart.

I wish to extend my profound thanks to all of these people, as well as to the individual writers, and to others who are not named but gave of themselves so that deadlines could be met and a story told.

. . . *R. James Ogden*

3

DEDICATED

To American Baptist congregations to which I have had the privilege of belonging, for it is the tension between the experience and gospel which they have given me and the values which shape so many decisions in the business of society that has made the question of integrity an important one for me:

The First Baptist Church of Burlington, Washington—where the question was that of moral and spiritual integrity;

The Lakeshore Avenue Baptist Church, Oakland, California, a number of college and university churches, and an Indian mission—where the questions were those of intellectual, vocational, and societal integrity; and

Central Baptist Church, Wayne, Pennsylvania—where the continuing question is one of life style integrity set in the context of a renewed sensitivity to the Spirit.

CONTENTS

I. PREPARING TO USE THIS STUDY SERIES
General Introduction

The Bible is a major source through which we can learn what it means to be persons who experience wholeness and fullness in life, what life style means for a Christian, and what the source of power in life is. This study series provides a focus upon those themes, looking closely at seven persons in the Bible as they struggle with the meaning of life, faith, wholeness, integrity, and salvation. The series arose out of a particular programmatic thrust among American Baptist Churches in the U.S.A., but the continuing questions of faith and life which it addresses know no denominational, national, or organizational lines.

What is an evangelistic life style?

What does it mean to become a whole person?

What does it mean to be a person of integrity?

Everyone seeks, again and again, to fulfill the potential which one knows one possesses—to experience the sense of wholeness which comes in discovering new depths of one's being and moving into new frontiers. The church has struggled in every age to translate the Good News—the Évangel—into words and actions which bridged the gap between the centuries of history, from wandering Hebrew tribes, through the birth, life, and death of Jesus and a first-century Christian community, to their own day. People in our day look for Good News and seldom find it in what they see around them. We need to know again the message of Good News, and we need to discover what it means in terms of a life style in our particular place and time. The whole society examines the meaning of and searches for integrity in a day when it has become the campaign promise of every politician. All of these are signs that the time is ripe for a people who express and share, in word and deed, the possibility of an evangelistic life style.

An Evangelistic Life Style

Putting the words "evangelistic" and "life style" together produces a strange-sounding phrase. They are not words we generally see together. Yet the very strangeness of the phrase may give it power, for it takes two things that we think we understand and requires us to reexamine them. Many of our images of evangelism have been shaped by mass revivals, the handing out of tracts, and programs of visitation evangelism. Each of these images has an element of truth. Too often, however, we confuse a particular evangelistic technique with the meaning of evangelism itself. The word "evangelism" comes from the Greek "euangelion" or Evangel, translated as "Good News," "Good Tidings," or "Gospel." This word, or its Hebrew equivalent, "basar," appears about 150 times in the Bible. It is frequently connected with "preaching" and "declaring" the Good News. Three times it is used to describe persons, "evangelists," messengers—persons who announce the Good News. *The Interpreter's Dictionary of the Bible* notes that "Word" is frequently used as a substitute for *evangelium,* so that "in the NT [New Testament] the gospel is called the 'word of God' (forty times), the 'word of the Lord' (eight times), or simply the 'word' (forty times). . . . The statistical evidence," the dictionary goes on to say, "shows that for the primitive church's understanding of the gospel the emphasis fell upon the fact that it was a divine communication. It is not, however, for this reason, thought of as a verbal statement primarily, but rather as an event which manifests its divine purpose. . . . The starting point of its proclamation is not what the people want to receive, but rather what goods God is offering to them." [1] The Old Testament background of "word" includes action as well as speaking and thinking.

The word "evangelism," then, deals with the core of our faith. It is what God has said to and done for us as it comes to focus in the death and resurrection of Jesus Christ, enabling us to link ourselves with the love of God. It is little wonder that the word "Gospel" or "Good News" has come to be used as a title for the stories at the beginning of the New Testament dealing with the life and work of Christ as the instrument of God's love. Perhaps evangelism is the word that can be used to describe all of God's activity in his relationships with humanity and this world—Good News. After all, is not that what God is to us?

"Life style" is a popular term today to describe "the personal manner in which each individual conducts his daily life." [2] We talk about leisure life style, urban life style, alternate life style, etc. There is

---

[1] O. A. Piper, "Gospel," *The Interpreter's Dictionary of the Bible* (Nashville: Abingdon Press, 1962), pp. 442-448, esp. pp. 444-445.

[2] Joffrey Dumazedier, *Toward a Society of Leisure* (New York: The Free Press, 1967), p. 228.

no single comparable word or phrase in the Bible, but to look at the words translated as "manner" or "way" is instructive. Among the Hebrew words translated as "manner" (in the King James Version) are words which are in other places frequently translated as "word," "law," and "judgment."[3] Two of these words, "torah" and "mishpat," according to N. H. Snaith, "came to be used for the declared word of God, and as such both became synonyms for righteousness (that which conforms to the nature and will of God). . . ."[4]

The Greek word most frequently translated as "way" carries the meaning of road, highway, and journey. It is a word of movement. It is the same word which is used by Jesus when he says, "I am the way, the truth, and the life." The writer of Hebrews speaks of a "new and living way."[5]

If we take any of these words to provide some biblical insight into the meaning of life style, the connections between evangelism and life style are obvious. Both are rooted in the "Word" of God. Both focus on the new possibility found in Jesus Christ. To enter into an evangelistic life style is to become a "living word," proclaiming the Good News in one's manner of life.

But too often we have not become a living word. Jacques Ellul challenges us when he says:

> . . . if we consider the life of Christians in our churches . . . they have no style of life, or rather, they have exactly that which has been imposed upon them by their sociological conditions: that is to say, by their social class, their nation, their environment, and so on. It is not their *spiritual* condition which affects their style of life: it is their political or economic condition. . . . This problem of the style of life is absolutely central; for it is at this point that the question of the integration of Christianity into the world, or at least of its creative power, will be most fiercely tested.[6]

Each of the biblical studies in this series is the story of the unique response of a person to God's activity in this world. They are stories of Good News and the journey of persons as the Word of the Lord becomes a living word in and through them.

Becoming Whole Persons

Modern social psychology gives us some insight into what it means to be a whole person. The identity of every person includes a very

---

[3] Robert Young, *Analytical Concordance to the Bible* (New York: Funk & Wagnalls Company, 1936), p. 643.

[4] N. H. Snaith, "Judge, Judgment," in Alan Richardson, *A Theological Word Book of the Bible* (London: S.C.M. Press Ltd., 1950), p. 117.

[5] Young, *op. cit.,* p. 1040.

[6] Jacques Ellul, *The Presence of the Kingdom,* trans. Olive Wyon (Philadelphia: The Westminster Press, first published by S.C.M. Press Ltd., 1951), pp. 146-147.

private dimension which is mysterious and rarely known to others, a social group dimension which grows out of the intimate relationships in which the person is involved, and a public dimension which is seen in the public roles of the person at work, as a citizen, etc. Put in a diagram, a person may be pictured as follows:

There is a sense in which this model of the person is alien to biblical thinking. As stated in *Becoming Good News People:*

> It comes out of contemporary Western social psychology. In biblical thinking, the person cannot be divided into segments. The very word "person" is rooted in what is basically a post-biblical Latin word, "persona," applied to actors, characters in a drama. In biblical thinking, the human being was one living being. Hebrew thought included the notion of corporate personality, where one's personality extended to include one's possessions, one's family, one's nation and, ultimately, one's God. Thus, it was possible for Israel to be both a nation and an individual. Somehow or other every individual *was* Israel. Similar thinking carried over into the New Testament (for after all the first Christians were Jews and thought like Jews) so that Paul speaks of us as being the body of Christ. When one member suffers, all suffer.
> While the Bible would not have sliced human beings up in this way, this view is a way of using twentieth century ways of thinking to return to the wholeness of biblical thinking. Like it or not, we do live in an age where our understanding of what it means to be a human being has enabled us to compartmentalize our identity. In American Christianity, in particular, we have tended to place religion in the private sphere and attempted to isolate it from our group relationships and our institutional roles.[7]

If we are to begin to grasp again a biblical understanding of the whole person, we cannot ignore what has happened. We need to identify the ways in which we have been divided up as persons and begin to get the pieces back together again.

Being whole, biblically, is closely linked with the Hebrew word "shalom" which we often think of as "peace" and the Greek word

[7] R. James Ogden, "Life Comes As Choice," in *Becoming Good News People,* ed. Richard M. Jones (Valley Forge: BNM, American Baptist Churches in the U.S.A., 1974), p. 14.

"teleos" which has to do with the end or purpose for which one exists. One is whole when one is fulfilling what is God's intention for his or her life. Wholeness is frequently related to healing. To be a whole person is to be a healthy and complete personality.

The Crisis of Integrity

The stories of biblical persons always portray a struggle to discover the meaning of faith in relation to specific historical circumstances, personal crises, and achievements, etc. If we are to respond with faithfulness to those stories, we must look not only at the world they faced but also at the crises of our times. This study series assumes that three crises dominate and shape much of what is happening in the world today—the crises of integrity, stewardship, and inter-dependence.

The specific studies included in this series were chosen to help us reflect on the meaning of integrity, but we should be aware, during the course of our study, of things we can learn from these stories about the life style implications of the other crises. The crisis of stewardship challenges us to recognize that we live in a world where some have much and many have little, where world famine lurks just around the corner, and where the end of all known supplies of life resources can be projected within a few generations. The crisis of interdependence may be traced to the abuse of power relationships and the classification of persons and things into superior and inferior, better and worse. "Whites are better than blacks." "People in positions of power should make all the decisions." "I can do whatever I please." These kinds of attitudes create a crisis of interdependence.

The focus here, however, is upon the crisis of integrity. Crises of integrity occur because we do not "have it all together" as persons. We are "split." Our private persons and our public persons are not in harmony. The word "integrity"—both biblically and in our day—has to do with being whole, perfect, and unbroken. Although the word appears only about sixteen times in the Bible,[8] the ideas of becoming whole, saved, reconciled, etc., are constant themes and remind us of the power of God to bind together that which has been broken or separated.

Each of the persons in this Bible study series reflects the way in which a person's response to God is interwoven with what is going on in one's whole life. To respond to God is to catch a vision of what integrity means—how and where it can be found. Integrity, however, does not come in the form of a sugar-coated pill. It comes in the midst of the struggle of day-to-day living where it must become embodied in the lives of human beings.

Thus, Nicodemus finds that Jesus challenges his role as a leader in the Jewish religion, and he must discover what it means to act with integrity among his close associates. We do not know the final outcome of his struggle, but we are convinced that he can never be quite the same after catching a glimpse of what a life of integrity can be. Job's whole conversation with his friends and with God revolves around his integrity. In arguing his case before God, he comes both to a new understanding of his own integrity and a new understanding of God. Ruth's act of integrity is a response to a family and the God of some foreigners, and it leads her to a new home. Her story gives us new insight into the power of God to use even a foreign woman, certainly not something which the people of her day would have expected, as a messenger of good news. Nehemiah must face what it means to act with integrity as a person of privilege relating to those who are struggling for survival in a devastated city. He must deal with the major economic and social problems of rebuilding a city. God confronts Peter with a situation which brings into question the integrity of obedience to certain religious laws. As a result, Peter discovers a new integrity which breaks down walls of separation between people. Jonathan must find and live out integrity as a leader of military might and as an intimate friend of David. His response brings to power a king who is remembered throughout history as a symbol of the nation of Israel. Barnabas expresses his integrity as a decision-maker in the early church. He is faced with new converts

[8] Young, *op. cit.,* p. 518.

who are not Jews, a suddenly converted old enemy (Paul) about whom the Jerusalem Christian leadership is uneasy, and a young missionary (Mark) who needs a second chance.

We, and those who know us best, are the only ones who can identify the points where we need to put together broken parts, where the issues of integrity are being faced in our lives. As we look at these biblical persons and share our insights in the supportive setting of the Christian community, it is our hope that a new light will be shed on our lives so that we come to a fuller understanding and experience of what it means to be whole persons—persons of integrity.

The Biblical Persons as Human Beings

The men and women of faith in this volume should be seen not simply as heroes and heroines but as real human beings struggling with who and what they are as children of God. They lived in different times and different places than we do. Their ways of life and ways of

thinking were often not the same as ours. The atomic bomb, the energy crisis, space travel, and most of the everyday conveniences we take for granted were unknown to them, just as most of us would not know how to build the walls of an ancient city or act in the presence of a first-century rabbi. The questions we bring to Scripture are not always the same as those being raised by people at the time of the original writing. Our question may not be, "How should Gentile Christians participate in the life of the church?" Instead, it may be, "What does it mean to be a Christian as a contemporary woman?" We may not ask, "How do I make sense out of my loss of family and wealth when I know I have done no wrong?" We *may* ask, "How do I find hope when the whole world I have known seems to be collapsing?"

Bible study, then, becomes a dialogue between the present and the past—between biblical persons and their stories and us. Since our questions may be different, we cannot expect to find "pat" answers. Answers that have life significance are usually stated in our own unique language to fit our own unique circumstances. We are often helped to discover answers, however, when someone says to us, "Well, this is what my experience has been." In this series, it is biblical persons saying to us, across the years, "This is what my experience has been in my journey with God." As we converse with them, they raise new questions and new perspectives which help us to discover God and to experience his meeting us in response to our own questions and life situations.

As we enter this dialogue, the following general questions provide a starting point for clarifying our response to the stories. More specific questions have been placed at the end of each chapter.

1. What do you like and dislike about the biblical person?
2. What decisions does the person make during the course of the story?
3. What other persons are important to him/her and how does he/she relate to them?
4. What is God doing in this story and what do we learn about his nature and action?
5. In what ways is this person struggling with questions of private identity, group relationship, and public responsibility?
6. What are the issues of integrity in this story?
7. What actions does this biblical person take that change his/her own life or the life of others?
8. What persons in today's world is this biblical person like?
9. In what ways are you like or unlike him/her?
10. What have you learned about yourself and in what ways have you been challenged to change as a result of studying the story of this biblical person?
11. After reading and discussing this story, what is your understanding of what it means to be a person of integrity? What does it mean for you to be a person of integrity?
12. What has this story contributed to your understanding of an evangelistic life style?

The biblical persons may seem like persons of unusual ability and faith, with whom we cannot identify. Their feelings of weakness and temptation, however, are repeatedly evident. Sometimes they seem to operate in positions of power—before kings, as leaders of nations, etc.—which seem beyond our reach. To discover what it means for us to be persons of integrity, to experience wholeness, in an evangelistic life style does not mean we must become carbon copies of one of these persons. We are to learn from them and let them challenge us to identify the points, wherever we live, where God is offering us wholeness and calling us to be persons of integrity.

Too often when we study the Bible, we fail to become personally involved and reach our own conclusions. The approach to Bible study in this series is one of involved interaction. Each reader is called upon to discover his or her own answers to questions about the meaning of wholeness, personhood, and integrity in an evangelistic life style. A final chapter has been included to illustrate a way in which such conclusions might be reached. Dr. Owens shares some of his own conclusions and encourages others to do the same. The series is not complete if each chapter is left as an isolated unit. The whole of the series needs to be brought together as a way of developing our own understanding of an evangelistic life style, discovering wholeness and integrity in our own life and experience. The same God who was at work in their lives is alive today, calling us, as he did them, to commit ourselves to his way, whether it be our first encounter with him, a challenge to discover and grow into deeper understandings of commitments already made, or a new decision point which we face in the continuing journey of faithfulness to him.

Group Structures and Process

No separate leader's guide has been prepared for this study series. Your group may or may not choose to have a formal leader. Whatever the form of leadership, the study of biblical persons can contribute the most to the development of an evangelistic life style when every person feels a strong sense of responsibility for what happens in the group. Therefore, general guidelines for the use of this study series are included as information useful to all group members.

There is no single "right" way to use this book, just as there is no single "right" way to do Bible study. Adapt it in the light of the situation in which you will be using it. Many of you will bring significant past experience in Bible study with you. Your greatest resource is within your own group and in the "Good News" which can come alive through the biblical stories you will be studying.

The following guidelines suggest some of the possibilities that might be considered in planning sessions around this study book:

1. Persons are most likely to be nurtured and grow when they are supported by a small group of persons who accept them, love them, and care about them. Bible study is most frequently effective when it takes place in the context of such groups. These are usually made up of eight to twelve persons where everyone can participate fully and share who he or she is as a person. The opinion and insight of every person in the group is essential, even if (or maybe especially if) it does not agree with your own. God has given each one of us unique insight, and it is only as we struggle together to understand what it is that God is doing in each of our lives that his truth emerges.

2. The scheduling of sessions will vary from group to group. Where possible, members of the group should commit themselves to the study group for a specific period of time. The study book is designed so that it can be used by a group meeting two to three hours one evening a week for seven or eight weeks,

or it can be adapted to a thirteen-week quarter in a church school curriculum.

Scheduling should allow time to examine the introductory overview so that the group has some common understanding of what the series seeks to do. There should be time, in a final session or two, to summarize what has been learned. The third section of the book, "Some Evangelistic Life Style Conclusions," suggests a way to go about the summarizing and offers the conclusions of one person as a discussion starter.

3. This book is designed for use by lay persons, with or without professional leadership. There may be a designated leader, or leadership may be shared, a different member of the group taking each one of the biblical persons and agreeing to do special preparation for those sessions.

4. Bibles, writing materials, and other familiar resources should be available. A one-volume commentary of the Bible, a Bible dictionary, and possibly a concordance would be useful tools. *The Interpreter's Dictionary of the Bible,* available in some church or public libraries, contains helpful articles on most biblical persons. Base your discussion on the biblical text as well as on the interpretations of the writers in this book.

5. Bible study will have limited effectiveness if it is something which occurs only during a specified meeting time once each week. Each participant should prepare for the group meeting by reading the study book section and suggested biblical passages, beginning to struggle with the general questions on page 14 and those at the end of the chapter which is being studied.

6. A variety of ideas about how to study the Bible are available. One resource is *Using the Bible in Groups* by Paul D. Gehris (Valley Forge: Judson Press, 1973). In fact, four sessions spent studying his little book could be a good way to move into this series. Other useful resources include *Guidelines for BIBLE STUDY* (a pamphlet produced for Key '73) and *Bible Study Groups* by Roy Pearson. Both of these may be ordered from Literature, Board of National Ministries, American Baptist Churches, U.S.A., Valley Forge, PA 19481, for 25¢ and 10¢ respectively.

7. The agenda for each session may vary. It is frequently useful to try different techniques, methods, and approaches. In general,

the meetings will probably cover the kinds of things that are shown in the following agenda possibility:

(1) Brief summarization by the leader for the week of the story of the biblical person being studied.

(2) Actual reading of selected biblical passages.

(3) General clarification and sharing.

(4) Sharing by several persons of work they have done in response to the study questions. Refer to the general questions on page 14, and also look at those at the end of each study.

> NOTE: It will not be possible to cover all the questions in any one session. Persons in the group should agree to focus on a limited number of them. One question to get the group started may be enough to carry the whole session.

(5) Discussion or other technique for group involvement.

(6) Drawing some conclusions about the meaning of integrity.

(7) Identifying two or three persons' concerns and/or commitments that members of the group wish to hold up in prayer as a result of the session.

(8) Time of prayer.

About the Writers

The writers of this Bible study series were chosen because of known competence as biblical scholars, their ability to translate the biblical stories into the life, times, and language of today, and because their lives demonstrate their own struggle with the kinds of questions raised in the series. Each contribution to this series is not only a conversation with a biblical person, but it is also the statement of a writer sharing the meanings he/she has found in the story being told. The style varies from study to study, reflecting the personalities and life circumstances of the various writers.

Rather than attempt to create an artificial uniformity, the differences in style are retained to illustrate a principle underlying these studies. No two persons will respond to the biblical stories in the same way. For us to express an evangelistic life style does not mean that we must all become alike and parrot the same words. Integrity will mean something different for each one of us. In each of these studies, we enter into the conversation between a writer and a biblical person as they seek to understand what it means to be faithful to God in our day. Becoming a part of that conversation means that we must finally "write" our own chapter, expressing what it is that has happened and is happening to us as we participate in the continuing journey of faith.

Since this study series seeks to understand biblical persons in their wholeness, looking at the history and context in which they lived, examining the issues to which they responded, etc., it is appropriate to see the writers in their wholeness as well. The brief biographical sketch about each writer deliberately avoids the usual description which focuses almost exclusively upon educational achievement.

CHARLES H. TALBERT, born in Mississippi into the family of a Baptist clergyman, is himself an ordained Baptist minister. He brings his biblical insights to us out of rich gifts as Professor of Religion at Wake Forest University, where his specialty is Christian origins. In addition to earning a Ph.D. from Vanderbilt University, he has engaged in post-doctoral studies both here and abroad and has authored a number of books and written many articles and reviews for learned journals. He keeps abreast of other fields as well, through membership in the Torch Club International, where the insights of professionals in a wide range of fields are shared. He is also a member of the Humanities Club on the Wake Forest campus, involving a similar kind of interaction. A major outlet for Dr. Talbert's interests and concerns is through dual church membership, in the Binkley Memorial Baptist Church, where his spirit is fed by great preaching, and in active participation with Mrs. Talbert in the Episcopalian church, which represents her heritage and whose liturgy equally meets a need of the human spirit. In both congregations he gives service in teaching and preaching in schools and conferences for both ministers and laity. He and Mrs. Talbert, who pursues the profession of diplomatic historian, share academic interests as well as sports, which they enjoy with their two children as much as the many demands on their time and energies allow.

KELLY MILLER SMITH was born in the Mississippi Delta. His ministry has been one of continuing presence in the racial crises of the nation, particularly as they first gained national attention in the South. Educated at Tennessee State University, Morehouse College, Howard University, Vanderbilt University, and Harvard, Dr. Smith is presently pastor of First Baptist Church, Capitol Hill, in Nashville, and Assistant Dean of the Vanderbilt Divinity School. He has served as president of the NAACP in Nashville. His church and an organization he founded led the nonviolent fight for desegregated schools in Nashville. His wife, Alice, teaches biology at Tennessee State University. The Smiths are the parents of four children.

PHYLLIS TRIBLE, in a disarmingly gentle manner, combines the life of a careful scholar and the life of a person who finds herself at the heart of one of the struggles which is shaking our society today. While her scholarly work is recognized by male and female alike, she has brought new life to the faith by encouraging women in their day-to-day existence to look again at biblical models. Educated at Meredith College, Union Theological Seminary, and Columbia University from which she received the Ph.D. degree, she is Associate Professor of Old Testament at Andover Newton Theological School. She is a student of Oriental traditions, in the interests of which she spent a year in Japan. She is presently studying in the Middle East, having been awarded the Younger Humanist Fellowship from the National Endowment for the Humanities for the year 1974–1975.

FRED E. YOUNG spans both rural and urban experience in American life. This is reflected in the fact that at Central Baptist Seminary in Kansas City he teaches courses in "The Old Testament and the City" and "The Old Testament in the Country." In addition to teaching, he is Dean of the seminary. Born on a farm in eastern Pennsylvania, Dr. Young comes from Pennsylvania Dutch stock. He and his wife, the former Sue Shellhammer, maintain Pennsylvania Dutch traditions at the dinner table, enjoying such treats as sauerkraut and shoo-fly pie. Ever since an early commitment to Jesus Christ as Lord and Savior, Dr. Young has been active in church life. He has studied at a number of major universities and received his Ph.D. degree from Dropsie College for Hebrew Studies in Philadelphia. Today, he is invited to lead church groups in Bible study. He believes that lay leadership development is a must in an alert Baptist church.

F. LENORE KRUSE chose for retirement living a spot just a stone's throw from the Schuylkill River where it winds along the side of Valley Forge State Park. Its wooded banks are the perfect place for long walks at sunrise with her two pups romping joyously ahead. Raised in city parsonages, schooled for her profession of Christian education in Philadelphia, St. Paul, and New York, and having served in the industrial centers of Detroit, Pittsfield, and Chicago, she never gets too much of the glory of God declared in earth, sky, and flowing stream. But the invisible yet grimly real fence around the area, penetrated by all too few minority people as yet, disturbs her peace and keeps her connected to movements whose objective is justice for all. The last fifteen years of her active career were spent with American Baptist National Ministries in association with Dr. Jitsuo Morikawa as he and his staff led American Baptists into new understanding of the meaning of evangelism, beginning with the Baptist Jubilee Advance where the seeds were sowed which are now coming to fruit in the Evangelistic Life Style Emphasis. Presently, her experience is being utilized part time in the Office of Developmental Planning and as a volunteer with the ELS staff at points where their overflowing responsibilities impel them to reach for an occasional helping hand.

SANTIAGO SOTO-FONTANEZ, according to a speaker at a banquet in his honor, "must be around a hundred years old. He served Central Baptist Church in Brooklyn for twenty years. He taught at Brooklyn College for twenty-two years. He has been director of Spanish work for the American Baptists, in New York, for fourteen years, and before that he served as a missionary teacher in Central America for seven years and as a pastor in Puerto Rico for another ten." His present work with the Board of Educational Ministries, American Baptist Churches, U.S.A., preparing and translating Spanish materials, adds three more years. The explanation is that Dr. Soto-Fontanez has always worked at two or three jobs at the same time. In the midst of this, he has also had time to work for a Ph.D. degree from Columbia University in New York. He has studied extensively in the classical languages—Latin, Greek, and Hebrew. Born in Puerto Rico, he has spent the last thirty years in New York City. His life work has been devoted to various forms of education for Hispanic clergy and laity, guided by his philosophy that "a minority has to be better educated than the majority in order to get ahead." Ana Soto-Fontanez, his wife, is president of the Hispanic Baptist Women's Association of New York.

OWEN D. OWENS, in carrying out his heavy responsibilities on the staff of the Board of National Ministries, American Baptist Churches, U.S.A., combines joyous love and stewardship of the earth with love of neighbor, thereby keeping body and spirit constantly renewed. A minister ordained in the Methodist Church, Dr. Owens was born and lived through his college years in Wisconsin, where he also pastored a church for five years. He earned his graduate degrees from Union Theological Seminary and Northwestern University, culminating in a Ph.D. degree from the Graduate Theological Union in Berkeley, California. His deep concern for and insights into the issues of ecology and justice inform his membership in groups such as the Sierra Club and the Society for the Scientific Study of Religion. They also undergird his work in National Ministries in developmental planning and the Evangelistic Life Style Emphasis, where he is involved both in the creation of program resources and specialized research in planning and organizational development. With his wife, Sharon, he is raising a family of two sons and a daughter with whom they live close to the good earth as they tend their large organic garden and enjoy frequent camping trips together.

R. JAMES OGDEN has long been interested in the Bible, theology, and the social sciences and how they relate to one another. Formal educational experience—including completion of work for a B.D. degree from Berkeley Baptist Divinity School and a Ph.D. from Northwestern University—has been interwoven with practical application among farm laborers, American Indians, and juvenile offenders. Coming from a semirural background, Dr. Ogden also enjoys gardening the organic way. He has been employed by the National Ministries of American Baptist Churches in the U.S.A. for the past six years, where he has worked at linking the concerns of planning and evangelism. His planning interests also find expression as a member of the Strategic Planning Committee at Central Baptist Church, Wayne, Pennsylvania. Dr. Ogden is married to the former Dorene MacArthur. She and their two children, Jonquil and Juliette, constantly remind him that life is loving, relaxing, and enjoying human relationships as well as studying, working, and writing.

II. THE BIBLICAL PERSONS

Charles Talbert brings us a study in a style which looks closely at the Scripture verse by verse and word by word. His treatment of Nicodemus reminds us of how trapped we become in the ways of thinking which are most common in our day. An encounter with Christ challenges us to move beyond those ways of thinking as it did Nicodemus. He is seen as a religious leader who senses the possibility of new life in the person of Christ. He is sympathetic to what he has seen, and it affects the way in which he relates to his associates. But we never know whether Nicodemus became a follower of the Way or not. Meeting Jesus raised for Nicodemus a whole series of questions about integrity in relation to power and position, his religious heritage, and his way of understanding the world. Charles Talbert poses a series of questions which help *us* look at those same questions in our own life and world.

Preparatory Reading: John 2:23–3:21; 7:45–52; 19:38–42

Nicodemus and the Challenge of Christ
by Charles H. Talbert

So accustomed are we to thinking of Nicodemus as the one who came to Jesus by night that it sometimes comes as a surprise to realize he is mentioned by name at two other points in the Gospel of John. All three passages are needed to catch John the Evangelist's estimate of Nicodemus as a person in relation to the life and ministry of Christ. To do so, we need to examine the passages in two groupings: (1) chapter 2:23–3:21, and (2) 7:45-52 and 19:38-42. At the same time, we need to understand a little of the way John the Evangelist viewed the world in which he lived and wrote, since this influences the way he tells the story. Brief glimpses of his perspective will be given in the course of the study.

John 2:23–3:21

The core of this passage is a threefold dialogue between Nicodemus and Jesus:
(1) 3:1-3, Nicodemus said; Jesus answered.
(2) 3:4-8, Nicodemus said; Jesus answered.
(3) 3:9ff., Nicodemus said; Jesus answered.

The third section of the dialogue shades off into a meditation or commentary by the Evangelist. It is impossible to say just where the boundaries are between Jesus' answer and the meditation on it.

The overriding emphasis in 2:23–3:21 is the nature of the encounter between Jesus and Nicodemus. On the one hand, Nicodemus started with a judgment about Jesus (3:2), but he wound up facing a judgment about himself. This development reflects something of the way the Evangelist viewed Jesus. He is not an object one can observe, evaluate from a distance, and about whom one then makes up his mind. He is rather an active challenge to one's self-understanding. Jesus is the one who questions our life style or orientation in living. On the other hand, Nicodemus found Jesus not only a challenge to his old world but also an enlightenment about the means to a new world, a new life style, and a different self-understanding. The first two parts of the threefold dialogue reflect the challenge presented by Jesus to Nicodemus; the third presents Jesus as the revealer of the means to new life.

Nicodemus Faces a Challenge to His Understanding of God (3:2-3)

The first dimension of John's description of Nicodemus emerges from the context. Chapter 2:23–3:21 belongs together with 2:13-22 as part of a Passover scene (2:13, 23) preoccupied with signs (2:18, 23; 3:2). "Sign" is a term, used in John's Gospel, for what we would call a miracle. In these two stories of the temple cleansing and the night visit of Nicodemus, Jesus was confronted by people who understood the clue to God's presence and activity in the world to be an extraordinary display of power. In the first story, Jesus faced a demand for such a display of power: "What sign have you to show us for doing this?" (2:18). That is, Jesus' actions in the temple could only be legitimate if he did them on God's authority. To claim God's presence in his activity, however, Jesus had to establish that fact with an extraordinary display of power, with a miracle. In the second story, Jesus gained a type of following on the basis of his signs: "Many believed in his name when they saw the signs which he did . . ." (2:23). In 3:2, Nicodemus appeared as spokesman for the many (2:23) who revered Jesus because they believed that his signs/miracles pointed to a link with God. For Nicodemus and the group he symbolized, *power* was the clue to where God's presence and activity (God's kingdom) were to be found in history. "Rabbi, we know that you are a teacher come from God; for no one can do these signs that you do, unless God is with him" (3:2). Where in the world is God acting? For Nicodemus, God was acting if and when there was an extraordinary display of power (sign/miracle). This dimension of Nicodemus's situation is focused in his comment in the first part of the threefold dialogue.

Jesus' answer in the first part of the threefold dialogue was a challenge. "Unless one is born anew [born from above], he cannot see the kingdom of God" (3:3). That is, without a radically new orientation Nicodemus could not perceive the kingly activity of God among men. In the thought forms of the Fourth Evangelist, there are two worlds: the upper world of light where God dwells and the lower world of darkness where men and women dwell. The present world that we touch and see and feel is characterized as darkness because it does not know God. People in the realm of darkness are earthbound. They live not only in this world of darkness but also for it and out of it. They belong to this realm. They are "from below." (See, for example, John 8:23.) Nicodemus was from below. Jesus said, however, that he must experience a radically new beginning "from above." Otherwise he would never perceive the activity of God that comes from above.

Trying to rethink the Evangelist's position in our thought forms is not easy, but it must be done. "He or she lives in an entirely different world from me." Have you ever said this of an acquaintance whose style of life you just could not fathom? Have you ever lived for an

extended period of time in another country and experienced culture shock? "It is another world!" What we mean in these two cases is that the whole orientation of someone else's life style is based on different assumptions and expresses strange values. So we think of such an orientation as a foreign realm. It is this type of situation that John describes in terms of two worlds, the upper and the lower. Since Nicodemus's orientation to life was from below, he could not see the reality of that life from above without a change so drastic it can best be described as a birth, a new beginning.

In Nicodemus's case his orientation from below expressed itself in his belief that the nature of God was essentially power. Wherever, therefore, he saw an extraordinary display of power, he assumed God was at work (3:2). Miracle was the evidence of God's presence. For Nicodemus, to be born from above meant, in part, for him to come to understand God in a new way. The Evangelist's commentary in 3:16-17 makes it clear that for Nicodemus to perceive God's kingly activity would mean understanding God as *self-giving love* ("God so loved the world that he gave his only Son") rather than as *sheer power*. From this point of view, the clue to God's activity in the world is self-giving love for others rather than mere miracle. Such a change in perception, however, requires a reorientation so radical that it can only adequately be described as a "new birth." Nicodemus found Jesus a challenge to his view of God.

> *Question:* Can you think of occasions on which you shared Nicodemus's assumption that the clue to God's presence is a marvelous display of power?

Nicodemus Does Not Understand Religious Language

Another dimension of John's description of Nicodemus is focused in the second part of the threefold dialogue. Jesus had just spoken of the necessity of a radical new orientation to life, the new birth (3:3). Nicodemus's response reflected his lack of understanding. "How can a man be born when he is old? Can he enter a second time into his mother's womb and be born?" (3:4).

The theme of misunderstanding crops up often in this Gospel (for example, 4:10-15; 6:41-42; 13:8-10, etc.). In terms of the author's thought world, one belongs either to the upper or to the lower world. Jesus was from above and spoke out of this orientation. Jesus' contemporaries, however, were pictured as being from below and thought in that framework. Hence when Jesus spoke, he was frequently misunderstood. His hearers understood in terms of the lower world, whereas Jesus spoke in terms of the upper world. This misunderstanding came about, in part, because of the use of terms which are ambiguous in their meaning. So the Greek *anothen* in verse 3 can mean either "from above" or "again," that is, "a second time." Jesus meant the former. Nicodemus understood the latter which, of course, was a ridiculous notion.

Nicodemus's plight in the second part of the dialogue was his failure to understand the nature of religious language. Religious language speaks about the upper world but must do so in terms of the lower world. For Nicodemus to understand the meaning of the language Jesus used, he must have experienced the reality of the upper world; that is, he must have been born of "water and the Spirit" (3:5). Whatever "water and the Spirit" mean in verse 5, verses 6-8 show that the Evangelist's emphasis is on the Spirit.

If we try to think with the Evangelist but in our own categories, an analogy comes to mind. What if we were color blind and were confronted by one who spoke to us of shades of color beyond our comprehension? Only language in terms of what we perceive as color-blind creatures could communicate, but it could speak only insofar as it pointed beyond itself. Ultimately only "seeing" color could make the language meaningful.

For Nicodemus to penetrate the language of revelation, he needed to experience a new dimension of reality, something that represented so radical a break with his past and present that it was spoken of as a "new birth." The night visit of Nicodemus to Jesus exposed his failure to grasp the meaning of religious language.

Question: Can you think of times in your life when religious language became meaningful after your religious experience had broadened or deepened?

Nicodemus Confronts the Question of "Ways and Means"

In the third part of the dialogue, the question of "how" comes to the fore. "How can this be?" (3:9) Nicodemus was asking, "How can my earthbound condition be remedied? What will enable me to have a new understanding of God? What will enable me to perceive the meaning of religious language?" The answer given points to the descent-incarnation/ascent-glorification of the Son. Verses 14-15 focus on the ascent-glorification. Being "lifted up" refers both to the cross and the ascension. Verses 16-17 focus on the descent-incarnation. God's sending of his Son is his gift of love to the world. It is because of the event of Jesus Christ that new birth is possible. How? On the one hand, the Son makes the Spirit available (cf. 7:39; 14:16-17, 26; 15:26; 16:7, 13-14; 20:22). On the other hand, the Spirit makes the Son meaningful (cf. 14:26; 15:26; 16:14). In these terms, the descent and ascent of the Son explain "how" these things are possible. The combination of the Word (incarnation) and the Spirit (the result of the glorification) makes possible the kind of radical new orientation to life that can only be described as a new birth.

Question: Does it make sense to you that believing in the Son can change the life of a person so much that it can be described as a "new birth"? In what ways have you come alive as a result of the Word and the Spirit as you find them described in the third chapter of John? How did it happen to you?

John 7:45-52 and 19:38-42

From the Fourth Gospel's description of Nicodemus, it is unclear if he is to be regarded as a secret disciple like Joseph of Arimathea (19:38) or as a representative of the best in Judaism, who regarded Jesus highly. Both possibilities will have to be kept in mind as we consider the description and evaluation of Nicodemus by the Evangelist in 7:45-52 and 19:38-42.

A Description of Nicodemus Among His Associates and as an Individual

These two passages are valuable descriptions of Nicodemus because they allow us to see his behavior with his associates and his action as an individual apart from group pressure.

Nicodemus belonged to a group called the Pharisees (3:1; 7:50). Ancient Judaism was diverse, just as varied as Christianity is today. Within the larger Jewish community with all its different persuasions, there were sects, such as Pharisees, Sadducees, Essenes, and Zealots. These sects were to ancient Judaism what the various religious orders, like Franciscans or Jesuits, are to the Roman Catholic tradition. Contrary to modern Christian folklore, the Pharisees were the most liberal and progressive group in the ancient Jewish community. It was to this group that Nicodemus belonged.

The Pharisees, involved in a plot to arrest Jesus at the Feast of the Tabernacles (7:32), lashed out at the officers who had failed to accomplish their objective. They asked, "Have any of the authorities or of the Pharisees believed in him?" (7:48). The Evangelist's view is that they had, but did not confess it lest they should be put out of the synagogue (12:42-43). It is possible, therefore, that when Nicodemus spoke, it was as one of the secret believers. He said, "Does our law judge a man without first giving him a hearing and learning what he does?" (7:51). He appealed to his peer group to act out of its own principles, to maintain its integrity. As devotees of the law, he said, "We must follow the law in judging a man. Give him a hearing." This of course was what Nicodemus had done in chapter 3. If he is regarded as a believer, then he was asking his peer group to do as he had done. Doubtless, he expected the same results. With a fair hearing, Jesus would make more disciples.

If Nicodemus is not regarded as a secret disciple but as a representative of the finest in ancient Judaism, then his appeal to his peer group has another meaning. He was reflecting a tolerance and fairness for those of a differing religious persuasion. He was doing so because the very basis for his religion (the law) demanded it (7:51).

Whether Nicodemus is regarded as a believer or not, it is clear that his personal values found some type of expression in his behavior among his associates. Unfortunately his strategy did not meet with success. His fellow Pharisees responded to his appeal to the law with another appeal to the Scriptures. "Search and you will see that no prophet is to rise from Galilee" (7:52). Both Nicodemus and the Pharisees appealed to tradition and the Scriptures in support of their position, much as we sometimes do today.

> *Question:* Can you see how your "new birth" has resulted in changed behavior in your relationship with your associates in your business or profession, or in the groups to which you belong?

Whether Nicodemus is regarded by the Evangelist as a believer or not, it is clear that when he was free to act as an individual divorced from his corporate responsibilities, his actions reflected his respect or reverence for Jesus. Joseph of Arimathea, a secret disciple, assumed responsibility for placing the body of Jesus in his tomb (19:38, 41-42). Nicodemus's function was to anoint the body, as was the burial custom of the Jews. Note the vast amount of spices! (19:39-40). Judas had been scandalized by one pound of perfume used for Jesus when he was alive (12:3-5). In his death, Jesus was treated in kingly fashion (cf. 2 Chronicles 16:14) by lavish expenditure of wealth. If Nicodemus was a secret disciple, one cannot help but wonder if this portrayal reflects a compensation for what was not done during Jesus' lifetime. If Nicodemus was a representative of the best in Judaism, this lavishness could only have been a compensation for his community's mistreatment of a "man sent from God."

Question: Are you aware of situations in your life where you have gone overboard in your expressions of individual piety (for example, in tithing, etc.) to compensate for your failure to live out your values in your corporate life (for example, work, school, social contacts)?

The Evangelist's Evaluation of Nicodemus and His Kind

The Fourth Evangelist's evaluation of Nicodemus was unfavorable because Nicodemus did not make a public acknowledgment of discipleship. If, on the one hand, he was one who did not believe in Jesus, John's words in 12:37-40 and 46-49 apply, as summarized in verse 48: "He who rejects me and does not receive my sayings has a judge; the word that I have spoken will be his judge on the last day."

If, on the other hand, Nicodemus was a secret disciple, John's words in 12:42-43 apply: "Nevertheless many even of the authorities believed in him, but for fear of the Pharisees they did not confess it, lest they should be put out of the synagogue: for they loved the praise of men more than the praise of God."

One problem faced by the church to which the Fourth Gospel was written was that of the exclusion of persons from the synagogue because of their confession of faith in Jesus (e.g., 9:22, 33-34; 16:2). Nicodemus may very well have symbolized for the Evangelist and his church the Jew who was also a Christian but who did not want to do anything overt that would lead to expulsion from the synagogue. The danger which such a secret disciple faces, from John's point of view, is that of estrangement from Jesus Christ. Here is the relevance of the passage in John 15 on the vine: "I am the true vine, and my Father is the vinedresser. Every branch of mine that bears no fruit, he takes away. . . . If a man does not abide in me, he is cast forth as a branch and withers; and the branches are gathered, thrown into the fire and burned" (15:1-2*a*, 6).

From the Evangelist's point of view, the true believer is one who, like the blind man of chapter 9, confesses what Jesus has done for him (9:25-33) even though it costs him (9:34). He it is who abides in Jesus and bears fruit. If, in 3:5, "water and the Spirit" refer to baptism by "water," then the outer and inner dimensions of the new life are in view. Baptism, in the early church, served the function of a public acknowledgment of discipleship. It is followed by a life of fruit-fulness, both in one's individual and one's corporate worlds. Nicodemus, from John's viewpoint, did not participate either partially or totally, depending on one's estimate of his status, in the reality Jesus made available. This character, therefore, is portrayed as a tragic figure in the Fourth Gospel. He was less than he could have been. He did not "get it all together."

> *Question:* Do you personally ever find it difficult to "get it all together" as a Christian? Do you think it is possible for a church's or a denomination's program to "get it all together"?

SHARING OUR INSIGHTS

Charles Talbert's study of Nicodemus raises a whole series of issues about the meaning of integrity and an evangelistic life style. Nicodemus was like so many people we meet in that he did not wear a sign saying, "I am a Christian," or "I am not a Christian." We do not know. The study clearly requires us to reflect on what it means to respond to Christ. In addition to reviewing the questions Charles Talbert has included in the study, you may wish to examine one or more of the following areas:

1. "Secret disciple"—think about those words. What do they mean? Was Nicodemus a "secret disciple"? Have you ever been one? Are there ever occasions when it is appropriate to be a "secret disciple"? Lack of integrity and secrecy seem to go together in our day. Could one be a "secret disciple" and be a person of integrity? Would an evangelistic life style ever be that of a "secret disciple"?

2. "A judgment about himself"—Charles Talbert notes that "Nicodemus started with a judgment about Jesus . . . but he wound up facing a judgment about himself." Jesus, he says,

"is . . . an active challenge to one's self-understanding." In what ways was Nicodemus's self-understanding challenged? In what ways is your own self-understanding challenged in this biblical study? In what ways do Jesus and the Good News challenge your self-understanding? What kind of self-understanding is involved in being a person of integrity?

3. "Expulsion from the synagogue"—following the Way of Christ in Nicodemus's time was sometimes costly. It meant being cut off by one's old friends. What is the cost of an evangelistic life style today? Is it likely to cut one off from anyone? Have you ever been afraid to state openly where you stood as a Christian because of what someone else might think or say? What is required of a person of integrity in such a situation?

4. "Religious language"—what is "religious language," anyway? Charles Talbert says that Nicodemus did not understand it. Are there words and phrases used in your church, in denominational publications, by your pastor, maybe even by yourself, that you do not understand? Do you very often speak in what you think of as "religious language"? Do people understand you when you do? What does it mean for a person to have integrity in his/her use of "religious language"? Are there times when its use is appropriate and other times when it is not? What kind of language should we use in an evangelistic life style?

5. "Display of power"—Charles Talbert says that "for Nicodemus . . . *power* was the clue to where God's presence and activity . . . were to be found. . . ." What kind of power was Nicodemus looking for? What kind did he find? What kind of power have you looked for from God? What does power mean to a person of integrity?

6. "Among his associates"—part of the story of Nicodemus involves what he said about Jesus to his associates. What do you suppose were Nicodemus's feelings during the discussion in John 7:45-52? Can you think of any similar experience you might have had with your own associates? Who are the people you consider your "associates"—your friends, the people you do business with, etc.? What is their attitude toward Jesus? What does it mean to be a person of integrity, as a Christian, in your relationships with them?

7. "New Birth"—birth provides us with an image of the beginning of a life. Physical birth is a rather abrupt change for the young life that is emerging into this world. Has anything ever

happened to you that involved such an abrupt and complete change that you could describe it as "new birth"? Does the "new birth" Jesus spoke about to Nicodemus always involve an abrupt change? What happens to the old person when "new birth" occurs? Part of what integrity means is being true to who you are. Does "new birth" mean that you have to give up all that you were as a person? Can you do that and be a person of integrity? Birth and growth are part of the same process. What kind of growth takes place in connection with a "new birth"? How do the images of birth and growth help us to understand, experience, and express an evangelistic life style?

8. "The best in Judaism"—one possibility considered by Charles Talbert is that Nicodemus was "a representative of the finest in ancient Judaism." Of course, all of the followers of the Way at the time this story took place, including Jesus himself, were Jews. Passages like the ones in John 3 have been used, over the years, to blame *all* Jews for the death of Jesus and to justify mistreatment of Jews. What was the relationship between Jews and followers of the Way in Nicodemus's time? What are the differences between the situation in that day and in ours? What is your understanding of and attitude toward "the best in Judaism" today? What does it mean for Christians to act with integrity toward Jews?

9. "Getting it all together"—to talk about "getting it all together" may be a more popular way of saying what the evangelistic life style emphasis and the Bible seem to mean by "integrity." Charles Talbert says that Nicodemus did not "get it all together." What are the things Nicodemus did not get together? What are the things you have a difficult time getting together? Do you feel, if you had them together, you would have more integrity as a person? Do you find clues in the story of Nicodemus about how to "get it all together"? What are the things you see an evangelistic life style trying to bring together? What does it mean for you to have integrity as a person with an evangelistic life style?

Kelly Miller Smith writes in a style which gives evidence of his deep identification with the human experience of suffering and doubt. He draws our feelings into the feelings of Job so that we cannot always tell which are which. The story of Job takes us to the very source of integrity, in God, and identifies those great enemies of integrity—religious pride and self-worship. It is the story of trouble and the discovery of wholeness in the midst of trouble.

Preparatory Reading: The Book of Job, with special attention to the following chapters:
1:1–3:26
19:1-29
31:1–32:22
36:1-33
38:1-41
42:1-6

Job's Inward Journey
by Kelly Miller Smith

Poor Job! It seemed that everything he held dear had sifted through his fingers like sand. At one moment the man was secure, happy, and content. In the next moment he stood stripped of all the things which made for his feeling of security, his happiness, and his contentment.

While we know the folly of making an idol of material things, we also know the folly of pretending that these things do not matter. Jesus did not say that man does not live by bread. Rather, he says that something else must be added—but bread is essential. Even that was gone for Job. With material things gone, a man could plan to work and catch up and perhaps get ahead again if he had his health. But that, too, was gone. Perhaps one's children could cover the loss. But what if they, too, were wiped out? This was Job's fate. Friends? They were there, but in some ways they became a burden for him.

Aha! Always there is God! When all else is gone, how comforting it is to know that God is there. So, Mr. Job, you can fall back on God. Tell him all about your troubles and be content again because he answers prayer. This is the testimony of thousands. Does not the psalmist (27:10, KJV) say

> "When my father and my mother forsake me,
> then the Lord will take me up"?

The matter is settled, then. Next case! But wait! How was that again? What did you say, Job? You lost WHO? Oh, no, not *HIM!*

> "Oh, that I knew where I might find him,
> that I might come even to his seat! . . .
> Behold, I go forward, but he is not there;
> and backward, but I cannot perceive him" (Job 23:3, 8).

Now what? With these crushing calamities, what can a person hope for? Who, pray tell, can put Humpty Dumpty together again? How is wholeness possible in this kind of situation? Or, is Job's situation so unusual that it has no meaning for contemporary man? Is this dreary story of calamities upon calamities just a storybook occurrence?

Granted our calamities are not always precisely the same as those which Job met, the fact that we are caught up in circumstances of crisis is undeniable. We must face the awesome task of searching for meaning and striving for wholeness in times and circumstances like these. Our contemporary crises plus the human situation raise some of the same issues which Job had to face.

Trouble Is Both Personal and Social

Whether we are talking about social crises or those that are personal is not as important an issue as it may appear. In the final analysis they cannot be separated.

Job may well have felt something of the depth of pain which black slaves knew when they sang "Nobody Knows the Trouble I See" and "Couldn't Hear Nobody Pray." So often tragic circumstances seem to isolate us from other human beings. Even those who are in trouble of various sorts seem not to be in the same situation as ours. And, in a real sense this is the case. Our trouble *is* our trouble. It is peculiar to us in the sense that it involves the peculiar circumstances of our lives.

Part of the pain of the crucifixion of Jesus was the pain of isolation. A good symbol of this isolation is the fact that when he prayed in Gethsemane his disciples went only so far. Then he was alone—alone with his agonizing cries, alone with his feeling of impending disaster, alone with his tears and wounded spirit.

The presence of other persons does not necessarily cure the pain of isolation. The fact is that their company sometimes increases the pain. Associates and companions who are by our side and giving a running commentary can become a part of the problem rather than its solution. This is not to say that the interest and concern of others should not be appreciated. Rather, it is to say that their concern does not always deal successfully with the problem of isolation.

Job was alone—even with the presence of his wife. He was alone although his friends were around. The progress of the dialogue underscores the fact that our hero was in his own world in spite of the claims and arguments of his associates. Their comments actually emphasized his aloneness in many ways. Had they remained away, or silent, his mental isolation would not have been quite so graphic. Their presence—while wonderful and well-intentioned—reminded him of the fact that he was alone with his thoughts and evaluations of the situation in which he found himself.

His decisions and conclusions, though made in a social context, were personal. Fractured, alienated, frail, and confused, he had to decide. From within the context of his faith and understanding, he had to deal with his situation. The pathetic complaint went,

> "Why is light given to a man whose way is hid,
>   whom God has hedged in?
> For my sighing comes as my bread,
>   and my groanings are poured out like water.
> For the thing that I fear comes upon me,
>   and what I dread befalls me.
> I am not at ease, nor am I quiet;
>   I have no rest; but trouble comes" (3:23-26).

From the vantage point of his isolation he encountered God—but inadequately. What a dilemma! Obviously, his hopeless situation could be fully and completely relieved only by God. His restoration to wholeness could be accomplished only by God. Yet, in his view, warped by hardship and despair, God was seen as the problem—the author of his troubles.

For a "good" man, this was a special problem. The expectation that God should reward belief (1:9) is not a thought in the mind and on the lips of Satan alone. It is often the spoken and unspoken concern of contemporary people as they assume the posture of religious persons. Beyond flowery words, do we really believe that

"Man's chief end is to glorify God and enjoy him forever"?

When we are caught in the vicious agony of exhausting crises, do we not really assess our religion in terms of the relief it brings? We are not interested at such a time in "disinterested" religion. From some quarters we are encouraged to "become religious" for the sake of something called peace of mind. God then becomes our tranquilizer. But from the interior of our personal situations we know that a superficial answer will not do. From inside ourselves the question thunders, "Why? Why? Why?"

There came for Job that unavoidable moment when he had to discover who he was in the light of certain realities. His wife, his friends, and his associates had their views, and they were rather forcefully presented to him. But the ultimate decision was his. It was crucial that he separate himself from them and decide where he stood. Step by step Job had to find his way back to God and to the deeper meaning of life. There were those shouting directions to him and perhaps this was helpful; but, finally, it was his journey. Although it was made graphic by outward circumstances, it was for him an inward journey—a journey inside himself. Says Howard Thurman, "For all of us are His children and the most crucial clue to a knowledge of Him is to be found in the most honest and most total knowledge of the self." [1] The shocking calamities reminded Job of a need that was there all of the time. He needed to come to grips with himself and his God. The need is universal but not always recognized.

Although the experiences of our hero were deeply personal, as we have been suggesting, they were also inescapably social. As soon as word reached his friends of misfortune, they felt involved and went to him. Not only did they go, but also they felt compelled to respond to the conditions. They responded with silence at first—then with

[1] Howard Thurman, *The Inward Journey* (New York: Harper & Row, Publishers, 1961), p. 40.

dialogue which was designed to help meet or at least interpret the situation. Neither an individual's suffering nor one's faith can properly be seen as personal only. One's personal faith has social meaning. One's relationship with God reflects itself in his or her relationship with other persons.

The first person to demonstrate some form of involvement with Job in his suffering was his wife. She had doubtless shared in some of the calamities which befell him. Those who died were her children, too. She shared in the property loss. Even as Job sat in indescribable agony, she was involved. We cannot be absolutely clear what was in the mind of "Mrs. Job" when she spoke to the condition, but she did demonstrate the fact that she was involved in his disasters. She gave her interpretation of the situation and of his hopelessness: "Do you still hold fast to your integrity? Curse God, and die!" (2:9). Give up the struggle. Your hardship dwarfs your integrity. You cannot possibly win. Throw in the towel. Or, was "Mrs. Job" trying to suggest suicide? Was it that she simply could not stand to see him suffer and wanted him out of his misery?

Whatever the case may be, this one thing is certain. She was not ready. She was of no real help to him in a severely critical time. This was one of those cases where the person who should have been closest was farthest away. At a time when he needed an understanding companion more than ever, this is what he had to put up with. He needed human companions whose presence would make a positive difference, and he needed the right kind of encounter with the *right* God.

There were the others—Eliphaz, Bildad, Zophar. They were there and they participated at their own levels. They came freighted with their religious clichés, their unyielding orthodoxy, their unmistakable biases. They were there, but they were more involved in pushing their wares than in trying to understand what Job was really facing and what his needs were. There is no wonder that Job cried out:

> "I have heard many such things;
>   miserable comforters are you all.
> Shall windy words have an end?" (16:2-3*a)*
> "How long will you torment me,
>   and break me in pieces with words?
> These ten times [or often] you have cast
>   reproach upon me;
> are you not ashamed to wrong me?" (19:2-3)

The personal and social nature of contemporary problems cannot be seriously doubted. There is the personal dimension which must be faced—ready or not! Then, the involvement of other persons in our lives is inescapable. Both these dimensions of the human situation, however, serve to underscore the deep need to meet God—on *God's* terms.

The Task of Locating God

God is involved throughout the story of Job. In the very first verse of the drama, this is evident. Job is introduced as "one who feared God." The first act shows a conversation between God and Satan. In fact, this is how it all started—with God and Satan talking about Job. Job and his companions never ignored the involvement of God both in what was then happening and in what was conceived as a possible remedy. But our hero was becoming aware of the fact that a new look at God was necessary. The God of beautiful phrases and narrow creeds simply was not sufficient.

Rooting their cries in certain crucial experiences, many have testified about their difficulty in finding God. Shailer Matthews, of another generation, asked the question which some raised: Has God been retired? Are our churches merely philosophical alumni associations? A few years ago some suggested that God's name could perhaps be found in the theological obituary columns. The prophet Isaiah referred to him as a God who hides, and Jesus quoted a psalm when he cried out from the cross, "My God, my God, why have you forsaken me?"

It must be said for Job that he was not willing to go on as if God did not matter. He threw up no impressive wall of empty claims. He frankly confessed that he had somehow lost his grip on God or he never had the proper grip to start with. It is natural for circumstances to arise when God seems to be missing in action. God does yield to the persistent probings of the honest seeker after him. He does finally show up when we face the reality of our need. But we must admit that the need is there.

How we lost him is another matter. Could it be that we have been so busy with the trappings of religion that we let him get away? The late Nels F. S. Ferre compared this with an umbrella which we place over ourselves to keep the sunlight of God from striking us with any force. Or it may be that we give ourselves such absolute credit for our successes that there is no room for God.

There were some errors in Job's quest for God, and we must guard against making them ourselves. For one thing, Job was not looking for God for the right reasons. There was no desire on his part to go before God "as an empty pitcher before a full fountain," as one black prayer expression has it. Rather, he was absolutely sure that he had all of the necessary answers; he simply needed an audience with God.

> "I would lay my case before him
> and fill my mouth with arguments.
> I would learn what he would answer me,
> and understand what he would say to me.
> Would he contend with me in the greatness
> of his power?
> No; he would give heed to me" (23:4-6).

In other words, Job was lacking in an openness to God. He was not at the moment in the frame of mind to say yes to God. He expected God to say yes to him. Job looked for God on his own terms. He looked for him for his own reasons. He had something that he wanted God to do for him. He needed him to approve his procedures and concepts. He needed God to back him up before his friends.

Involved in Job's quest is the fact that he was looking for the wrong type of God. He had some notions of God which he expressed earlier in the drama. One fears that this is part of the reason for our failure to find God even when we search. We just may be looking for a God who does not exist—perhaps a "peace of mind" God who is around for our use whenever we desire. We may be looking for a gift-bearing God or a God who resembles ourselves.

God of the Whirlwind

The drama moves on toward its exciting climax. We have listened to the abrupt words of Job's wife, the critical judgments of Eliphaz, Bildad, and Zophar, and the agonized cries of Job. The wise words of Elihu (36:7-10, 13, 26-28) helped to prepare Job psychologically and theologically for an unforgettable encounter with God. And then, God himself broke the silence.

How would God make manifest his presence? Sometimes he speaks through the unspeakable glory of nature. Often through history, we have heard his voice issuing forth. From the Bible and in a multitude of other ways his voice is heard. But it is written:

> God moves in a mysterious way
> His wonders to perform;
> He plants His footsteps in the sea,
> And rides upon the storm.[2]

The *storm?* Not the multicolored rainbow, not the golden radiance of

[2] William Cowper, "God Moves in a Mysterious Way," *Christian Worship, a Hymnal* (Valley Forge: Judson Press, 1953), p. 162.

the morning sun, not the "still, small voice," or the voice of thin silence? Not this time. To match the storminess of Job's experiences, God spoke through the storm—through the whirlwind.

> Then the Lord answered Job out of the whirlwind (38:1).

So, sometimes our storms may be vehicles for the voice of God. Sometimes the experiences which we dread most become the means by which God speaks to us. So, when troubles come, it is well to listen carefully to the disturbing turmoil, for there may be a message there.

The first necessity is to get things in perspective. Let us understand who is who. Who must the questioner be? True, a human being is a question-asking, answer-seeking animal. But God is the ultimate questioner. The penetrating, persistent questions come from him. How do we fare when God does the questioning? One thing Job could tell us is that God's questioning helps us to see ourselves more clearly. Job thought he would scale God down to size, but not so. When God was done questioning Job, *he* was scaled down to size. It then became clear that he not only did not know the answers—he also did not know the questions. God thunders,

> "Who is this that darkens counsel by words without knowledge?" (38:2)

What could Job do but tremble? He then began to feel some of the awe, the humiliation, one must feel in the presence of God. Remember when Isaiah met God, he cried out, "Woe is me! for I am undone!" (Isaiah 6:5, KJV).

The fact that God showed up is a message of great power. He appeared, however, in his own time and manner. But his presence spoke eloquently. Speaking as he did out of the whirlwind and giving a poetic interpretation of the creation story, God revealed to Job both his greatness and his love.

The message was clear: Job was not guilty of moral delinquency as his friends had accused him. Rather, his was a problem of religious pride and self-worship. God overwhelmed Job with a graphic reminder of how God functions in ways in which the hero of the drama could not.

Response to the Divine Encounter

One must do something. There has to be a response when God speaks. Job's response included the oft-repeated words:

> "Therefore, I have uttered what I did not understand,
> things too wonderful for me,
> which I did not know" (42:3).

Job gained a new outlook on his troubles. These had pretty much shaped Job's approach to God. Trouble should never so possess us that our every conversation is about our problems. At first, trouble was the platform upon which Job stood for all that he said. It was the overwhelming fact. The divine encounter became the occasion for his stretching beyond this flimsy platform to touch the very hand of God. Through all of this he was able to see God as he never had before.

> "I had heard of thee by the hearing of the ear,
> but now my eye sees thee" (42:5).

And this meant he saw himself in a new way.

Poor Job? Not now! He had overcome. He had learned the meaning of wholeness. He was aware of his human situation, but he was also aware of the divine resource, and he could make it. So can we.

SHARING OUR INSIGHTS

The story of Job challenges us to take a look at our understanding of integrity, to take an "inward journey," and to come face to face with God. He causes us to reexamine what it is we value in life and why. "Troubles" are portrayed in a depth we seldom see; yet we find the possibility of a new outlook on trouble. Profound psychological and theological themes become the basis for clarifying our own insights and identity.

1. "Calamities"—Job was a person who knew calamities. Do you know any persons who have gone through similar experiences? What calamities have you known? Have you ever been as low as Job seemed to be? What happened to put you there? Kelly Miller Smith suggests that "when troubles come, it is well to listen carefully to the disturbing turmoil, for there may be a message there." Have any messages ever come to you out of calamity? What kind of message came to Job? What does it mean to be a person of integrity in the midst of calamity?

2. "Inward journey"—Dr. Smith talks about "the pain of isolation," but he also talks about Job's isolation forcing him to take an "inward journey." Job "had to discover who he was. . . ." Who are you in your most private moments? Have you ever felt totally alone? What did you find out about yourself? Dr. Smith says that God's questioning helps us "to see ourselves more clearly." What kinds of questions does God ask you when you are alone? What does it mean to be a person of integrity in one's innermost privacy?

3. "Well-intentioned"—Kelly Miller Smith talks about the presence of Job's "comforters" as "well-intentioned" but not helpful. Have you ever felt your loneliness increase when a well-intentioned friend tried to help? Have you ever felt helpless when trying to comfort a friend? What kind of help did Job need? What kind of help can we offer to people who are "troubled"? What does it mean to act with integrity in "comforting" someone like that?

4. "Religious pride and self-worship"—at the heart of Job's problem was his self-righteous sense of being a "good" man. "Let me be weighed in a just balance," he says, "and let God know my integrity!" (Job 31:6). He expected God to reward his belief. Have you ever had similar feelings? What did Job finally find out about integrity? Can you identify ways in which "religious pride and self-worship" are part of your life? What is God saying to you about your own integrity?

5. "Peace of mind"—Kelly Miller Smith talks about a God who becomes our "tranquilizer." What is it that you are looking for from God? Are there times when you cry out for God to bring you peace of mind? Do we find comfort in the God we see in the Book of Job? Does the God you know seem to be the same God Job knew? Does having integrity mean having "peace of mind"?

6. "A new look at God"—Dr. Smith movingly portrays Job as one who had "lost his grip on God." He could not find him because he was looking for the wrong God in the wrong way. Have you ever felt like you had lost God? What kind of a God were you looking for? What were your attitudes and feelings? Did you find him? Where and how? What can we learn from Job about finding God? What did finding God have to do with Job's integrity?

Phyllis Trible approaches the Bible as a source of living
stories and brings us into the drama and agony and
movement of those stories. In retelling the story of Ruth,
she stresses the themes of emptiness and fullness or
wholeness. She helps us see the drama of women of action
in a male-dominated world. She illuminates the meaning
of risk in the life of faith. Ruth's faith is seen as radical in
the sense that it goes to the very center of her being,
enabling her to risk and change and move into an
uncertain future.

Preparatory Reading: The Book of Ruth.

The Radical Faith of Ruth
by Phyllis Trible

As a work of art, the Book of Ruth presents a highly developed
theological posture. In it we see women struggling for survival in an
environment which is alien and sometimes hostile to them. They have
no time and no place in their lives for sweetness and light. They have
no guarantees from God or from anybody else that life will turn out
well if they "just have faith." They themselves must make radical
decisions; they must risk bold, even shocking, acts for the sake of
survival and the hope of blessing. They know hardship, danger,
insecurity, and death. All of which is not to say that the book is a
tragedy. Though it begins in deep despair, it surges forward to well-
being.

Four scenes mark the outlines of the story. These scenes have a
circular pattern whereby the fourth returns to the concerns of the
first. Within each scene and overlapping among the scenes, opposites
intertwine to highlight tension and to effect its resolution.

Chapter 1 is the first scene. It begins with a sojourn in Moab (1:1)
and ends with the conclusion of that stay (1:22). It commences with a
famine in Bethlehem and concludes with the end of that famine, the
time when the barley harvest begins. Throughout this scene, famine
alternates with fullness; emptiness alternates with wholeness; death
alternates with life.

There is famine in the land of Judah. A full, complete family leaves that emptiness to live for a time in the country of Moab: a husband named Elimelech, a wife named Naomi, and their two sons named Mahlon and Chilion. The completeness of this family begins to dissolve immediately with the death of Elimelech (1:3), but the story moves swiftly to overcome this sign of emptiness by reporting that the two sons take Moabite wives named Orpah and Ruth (1:4). Their marriages signal the possible continuation of the family line. Yet we know the comfort of this news for only one verse before we read that the sons also die (1:5). Without husband and sons, Naomi hears that Yahweh (the Lord) has sent food to the people of Judah. So she begins the journey homeward. Once as a family of fullness she left her native land because it was a place of famine. Now as a family of famine she returns to that home because it is possibly a land of physical fullness.

The daughters-in-law begin the journey also, only to be discouraged by Naomi. Three times she commands them to return to their mothers' houses, and each time she links this order with the necessity of their finding husbands (1:8-9, 11, 12-13). If life is to have any fulfillment for these young women living in a male-dominated society, then they must remarry. Their chances are far greater in the native land of Moab than in the foreign land of Judah. At the

beginning of her words, Naomi invokes the loyalty and graciousness of Yahweh in urging Orpah and Ruth to return home; at the end she cites her harsh treatment from Yahweh as a bitterness which she does not wish upon them. These references to deity frame the advice to her daughters-in-law, although nowhere in the scene does God intervene in a direct way. The human condition itself reveals divine activity.

Knowing this situation, the two women choose. "Orpah kissed her mother-in-law, but Ruth clung to her" (1:14b). The decision of Orpah is sound, sensible, and secure. Our storyteller does not linger over it. He or she reports it simply, with neither praise nor blame. Naomi points to it as the proper decision, the one to be followed: "See, your sister-in-law has gone back to her people and to her gods; return after your sister-in-law" (1:15). Thereupon Orpah fades from the story altogether. Very briefly she is present as a model of the sane and the reasonable; she acts in accordance with the structures and customs of society. Her behavior contrasts with that of Ruth. Orpah does the expected; Ruth does the unexpected.

As participants in the story, we ought to ponder what it means to continue. Some among us would choose the way of Orpah and not the way of Ruth. We would do the proper and the expected. We would be the daughter who stays at home rather than the one who leaves her mother's house to dwell in an unknown land. If we follow Orpah, the story does not scold us. It simply leaves us behind. The movement of faith lies with Ruth (and Naomi), not with Orpah.

The decision of Ruth makes no sense. Leaving the security of home, she seeks insecurity abroad. Offered possible fullness in Moab, she chooses certain emptiness in Judah. She gives up the familiar for the strange. In her culture one does not make such choices. To be sure, Abraham does, but then he has a call from God (Genesis 12:1-5). Divine promise motivates and sustains his leap of faith. In addition, Abraham is a man, with a wife and other possessions to accompany him. Ruth stands all alone; she possesses nothing. No God has called her; no deity has promised her blessing; no human being has come to her aid. She lives and chooses without a support group, and she knows that the fruit of her decision may well be the emptiness of rejection, even of death. Nevertheless, she decides without reason or explanation: "Entreat me not to leave you or to return from following you; for where you go I will go, and where you lodge I will lodge; your people shall be my people, and your God my God; where you die I will die, and there will I be buried. May the Lord do so to me and more also if even death parts me from you" (1:16-17). These are not sentimental words for a marriage ceremony. A woman alone commits herself to another woman, to a strange land, to a foreign people, and to a God whom she knows as the bringer of death.

Naomi protests no longer. The two females journey to Bethlehem. Their arrival arouses the women of that town, who ask, "Is this Naomi?" (1:19). Then that emptiness which has continued to triumph throughout this scene overwhelms in the reply of Naomi to their question: "Do not call me Naomi, call me Mara, for the Almighty has dealt very bitterly with me. I went away full, and the Lord has brought me back empty. Why call me Naomi, when the Lord has afflicted me and the Almighty has brought calamity upon me?" (1:20-21). Famine on all levels has so overpowered and exhausted Naomi that her words do not even allow for the presence of the daughter-in-law who has chosen to accompany her. Naomi experiences life as utter, total, complete emptiness—from famine on a physical level to famine on a familial level to famine at the very core of her existence. "I went away full, and Yahweh has brought me back empty."

Just as scene one is drawing to a close in the deep anguish which Naomi has sounded, there is a cautious movement toward well-being in the concluding comment of the storyteller (1:22). Naomi is not alone. Though she does not acknowledge it, Ruth the Moabite, her daughter-in-law, is with her. Moreover, these two people have come to Bethlehem at the beginning of the barley harvest. The possibility of fullness in the harvest challenges the overpowering presence of famine.

The narrator opens scene two (2:1-23) by introducing Boaz, who is a contrast to the males of scene one. Although named, Elimelech, Mahlon, and Chilion speak not at all and pass away very quickly by death. Boaz himself is to assume a major role in the story. To emphasize his importance, his introduction occurs several verses before he actually appears.

Action in this second scene begins with Ruth. She suggests and initiates a plan to provide food for herself and Naomi: "Let me go to the field, and glean among the ears of grain after him in whose sight I shall find favor" (2:2). If these women live in social and familial famine, they need not yield to physical hunger. So Ruth sets forth to glean in the field. We read that "she happened to come to the part of the field belonging to Boaz" (2:3). It is an appropriate expression, "she happened to come," suggesting chance and accident, but at the same time these words hint at another possibility. While the incident occurs without reference to God, divine purpose is hidden within it. In a subtle way we see the coming together of opposites: chance is caused; the accidental is the intentional.

Immediately Boaz spots the strange maiden in his field and asks for an identification. He is kind to Ruth, promising her food, drink, and protection (2:5-9). She is puzzled that he should show such concern for a foreigner (2:10). But Boaz is a true child of Israel, who knows that Israel herself lives as a stranger and sojourner in the world. Indeed, Israel had her beginnings in the foreigners Abraham and Sarah, who journeyed to a foreign land to become channels of blessing for all the families of the earth (Genesis 12:1-5). These ancient traditions echo in the reply of Boaz to Ruth. He describes her as one leaving her father and mother and her native land to come to a people whom she did not know (2:11). The words remind us of Ruth's own decision in scene one to leave the known and to choose the God of Naomi (1:16-17). Boaz prays that Ruth be given a full reward by Yahweh, the God of Israel, under whose wings she has come to take refuge (2:12). Thereupon he commands his servants to pull out sheaves from their bundles for Ruth to glean.

Scene two closes with Ruth reporting to Naomi the experiences of the day. It was a time in which famine yielded to food, the stranger became the friend, and the accidental mirrored the intentional. Blessing happened when Ruth dared to go out into the fields, risking rebuke and molestation. The outcome of that occasion is sufficient to soften somewhat the bitterness of Naomi. For the first time she speaks concretely of the loving loyalty of Yahweh, who has not forsaken the living or the dead (2:20), and she approves the plans of Ruth to continue work in the field of Boaz. (2:22).

The structure of this ending parallels the conclusion of scene one, while its content differs significantly. In both scenes words of Naomi complete the dialogue (1:20-21 and 2:20, 22). At the end of scene one, Naomi is overwhelmed by the emptiness of life and by the calamity which the Almighty has brought upon her. She knows only bitterness and sorrow. At the end of scene two, she hints at a possible reinterpretation of her past in light of the present blessing of Yahweh which has come through Boaz. She acknowledges kindness and hope. Yet in both scenes her speeches are not the final word. That word belongs to the narrator. Whereas in scene one he or she struck a note of well-being with the phrase "the beginning of the barley harvest," here in scene two the narrator reverses that note with the phrase "until the end of the barley and wheat harvests." The phrase is a warning, because the end of the barley season may mean the return of famine and emptiness. If present kindness has softened past harshness for Ruth and Naomi, their future is still uncertain. Thus at the conclusion of both scenes one and two, the narration is in tension with the dialogue; the storyteller is in tension with the characters. And the readers (or hearers) are left in suspense.

Naomi is the verbal link between scenes two and three (3:1-18). The last to speak in scene two, she is the first to speak in scene three. Having become aware of the kindness of Boaz, she begins now to act upon it. Naomi moves from being the receiver of calamity to becoming the agent of change and challenge. She does not wait for matters to take their course or for God to intervene with a miracle. Instead she proposes to her daughter-in-law an outrageous scheme, dangerous and delicate. Its context involves two women trapped in a male-dominated society, having to manage their own lives and destinies. But men do not make decisions for *them*. These women come into their own as female models, acting independently, decisively, and daringly.

Naomi's plan is this: At night Ruth will go down alone to the threshing floor where the men are eating and drinking in celebration of the harvest. After Boaz has satisfied himself with food and drink and has lain down to sleep, Ruth will approach him, uncover his "feet" (genitals), and lie there. The proposal is clear and shocking. We wonder how a man of Israel will respond to this bold action on the part of a woman. The very first words of Boaz do not tell us. Discovering a woman at his "feet," he asks, "Who are you?" (3:9).

Ruth's answer is direct: "I am Ruth, your maidservant; spread your skirt over your maidservant, for you are next of kin" (3:9). Her reply is also subtle, for she is calling upon Boaz to make good on his prayer for her blessing. In scene two, Boaz praised her in language that reminds one of Abraham's leap of faith, and he prayed that a full reward be given her "by the Lord [Yahweh], the God of Israel, under whose wings you have come to take refuge!" (2:12). The word translated *wings* in 2:12 is the same word translated *skirt* here in 3:9. Thus Ruth is challenging Boaz to be the occasion and instrument of divine blessing in her life. She is saying in effect that Boaz himself has the power to bring about the "full reward" which he wishes the God of Israel to give her. The refuge and blessing symbolized by the "wings" of Yahweh can be made real by the "skirt" of Boaz. The man who spoke this prayer for her is himself capable of fulfilling it.

Having taken the initiative, this woman awaits the response of the man. Relaxation of suspense comes briefly when Boaz blesses Ruth by Yahweh and promises to do all that she asks (3:10-11), but it fades quickly when Boaz mentions a kinsman nearer than he who must be asked first to "do the part of the next of kin" for Ruth. The precise meaning of this phrase is not clear and thereby it increases suspense. The words seem to waver between promise and postponement. In the morning Ruth departs, with Boaz protecting her from recognition and providing her with food. "You must not go back empty-handed to your mother-in-law" (3:17), he says, as the theme of emptiness-fullness surfaces once again in the story.

Naomi asks how her daughter fared and then gives her response to the situation: "Wait, my daughter, until you learn how the matter turns out, for the man will not rest, but will settle the matter today" (3:18). Having introduced scene three by plotting a dangerous mission, the aged woman concludes it now by counseling a patient wait. As in preceding scenes, her words complete the dialogue of this one also. But in this scene there is no final word by the narrator. Its absence removes the tension between author and characters, between narration and dialogue. The story is moving toward resolution.

These final words of Naomi in scene three are also her last speech in the book. The possibility that Ruth may find a husband in Boaz satisfies Naomi's original concern, which appeared in her very first speech in scene one (1:9). In this sense her function in the story is completed. Moreover, this woman who began as the voice of sorrow and sadness, of bitterness and suffering, of famine and emptiness approaches now the threshold of fulfillment and joy. Her voice fades. She steps aside while the story continues. Ruth steps aside also. Her bold actions for the sake of survival and the hope of blessing complete her contributions. Although both women are present at the conclusion of scene four, neither speaks there. The drama ceases to be their story and becomes the story about them.

The fourth scene (4:1-17) begins with a public gathering at the gate of the city where business and legal transactions take place. Boaz controls the action. In contrast to preceding scenes, where women have dominated, the characters are men. The appearance of the nearer kin occurs seemingly by chance. Passing the gate, he is invited to sit down. The casualness of this meeting clouds the purpose behind it. The situation is a variation upon the theme presented in scene two where Ruth "happened to come to the part of the field belonging to Boaz" (2:3). Now the nearer kin happens to come to a meeting planned by Boaz. His chance appearance suggests a hidden cause.

At the request of Boaz, elders of the city sit as judges and witnesses to the matter at hand (4:2). In measured, deliberate fashion Boaz talks to the next of kin (4:3-4). His speech contains surprises. He starts with new information, saying that Naomi wishes to sell land which belonged to Elimelech. (Apparently at some time in ancient Israel, widows might inherit the estates of their husband, even though Hebrew laws known to us do not allow for this possibility; compare Numbers 27:8-11.) Boaz offers this unnamed kinsman the opportunity to redeem the land. Redemption of property does not necessarily mean absolute ownership. Instead, it is a way of keeping land within a general family group. Redemption may amount to absolute possession and thus be profitable for the buyer, as long as no legitimate heir appears to reclaim the property.

The next of kin agrees readily to redeem the land which Naomi is selling (4:4), but the significance of this matter is yet to come. The fate of the land is inseparable from the future of Ruth the widow. If she remarries and has a child, the land will belong to that child, not to the kinsman. By delaying information about Ruth, Boaz exposes the motives and character of the kinsman. When the unnamed one learns about Ruth, he withdraws his offer to redeem the land because it might endanger his own inheritance (4:6). In other words, he agreed to redemption for personal gain and not out of concern for the name of the dead. His own words reveal his selfish interest. There is no stated judgment upon him. But a subtle judgment is present in his very lack of a name. Refusing to restore the name of the dead to his inheritance, this man himself has no name.

The shoe ceremony which follows secures the right of Boaz to buy the land, to marry Ruth, and thereby to "perpetuate the name of the dead in his inheritance" (4:7-10). Witnessing this transaction, the people and the elders offer a prayer about Ruth which compares her to the ancient mothers—Rachel, Leah, and Tamar (4:11-12). These comparisons recall other parallels between Ruth and Abraham (1:16-17; 2:11). All of them together place Ruth the foreigner solidly within the history of Israel. She is there both as a bearer of children and as a model of the radicality of faith.

The prayer of the people concludes the public transaction. One brief verse reports that Boaz married Ruth and that Yahweh "gave her conception and she bore a son" (4:13). The privacy of their union is sandwiched between public gatherings which, on the one side, legitimate the union and, on the other, celebrate it.

At the celebration no men are present (4:14-17). Women of Bethlehem, first stirred by Naomi's return from the land of Moab in scene one, reappear to introduce and to conclude the last episode. They commence it with a blessing of Yahweh, and they address their words to Naomi, the one who had told them earlier that Yahweh brought her back empty. Now at the end they answer her: "Blessed be the Lord [Yahweh] who has not left you this day without next of kin" (4:14). The coming of a grandchild transforms death into life, emptiness into fullness. But these women say something even more striking. Pointing to Ruth as the mother of the child, they remind Naomi that Ruth loves her and indeed that Ruth is more to her than seven sons (a powerful assertion in a male-dominated society). Perhaps their words gently scold Naomi, who, upon her return from Moab, did not even recognize the presence of Ruth with her as a sign of blessing. Naomi affirms and participates in the blessing as she takes the child, lays him in her bosom, and becomes his nurse. The women even speak of the child as having been born to Naomi, and they conclude the scene by naming him Obed.

All in all, a work of art has unfolded a story beginning in deep despair and surging forward to blessing. Though the giver of blessing, God does not intrude in the story by words or by miracles. The progression to well-being comes primarily through the brave and bold decisions of women. They seek food in the face of famine, life in the midst of death, and wholeness in the presence of emptiness. Ruth herself is the model of a radical faith which dares to risk all. She knows what it means to live without support and without promise. She gives in neither to self-pity nor to a religiosity which refuses to see reality. She exemplifies integrity, even though (or perhaps because) her wholeness challenges custom and risks disapproval. It is indeed fitting that later generations should remember this foreign woman in the genealogy of Jesus the Christ given in Matthew (see 1:5).

SHARING OUR INSIGHTS

The story of Ruth challenges us to examine the relationship between faith and the customs of our day. In the story of Ruth, these relationships are set in the context of a flow from emptiness to fullness in life, providing insight into the source of wholeness and meaning in life. Phyllis Trible's style draws us into the story all along the way. Several themes seem especially to lend themselves to further reflection as we move between the story of Ruth and our lives.

1. "The expected and the unexpected"—Phyllis Trible contrasts the behavior of Ruth with that of Orpah. One conforms; one risks. In what ways are you like Orpah and in what ways are you like Ruth? What customs do you accept that maybe you should challenge? What risk did Ruth take? Have you ever been called upon to risk something for the sake of your faith? Are there any risks to which you are being called now? What does it mean to be a person of integrity in the tension between conformity and risk?

2. "The theme of emptiness-fullness"—the story of Ruth and Naomi alternates between experiences of emptiness and fullness. What is the nature of the emptiness and the fullness at various points in the story? Have you ever felt "empty"? What was the nature of your emptiness? What is the source of fullness in the story of Ruth and Naomi? How is it discovered? What are your experiences of fullness and where do they come from? What does all this have to do with being a person of integrity?

3. "Women in a male-dominated society"—Phyllis Trible stresses the degree to which this is a story about women who refuse to fit stereotypes and accept predetermined roles. Why did they do this? What motivated them? What made them able to act the way they did? Are there roles in life that you have accepted without thinking? What does it mean to be a person of integrity in relation to roles defined for you by society?

4. "Without a support group"—Phyllis Trible declares that "Ruth stands alone. . . . She lives and chooses without a support group." How do you feel about that interpretation of the story? Have you ever felt all alone in making a decision? Phyllis Trible also points out the relationship of love and interdependence between Ruth and Naomi, although they did not always recognize its value. What persons do you know whose support

you may not have admitted? What is the nature of the support Naomi and Ruth gave each other? What does being persons of integrity have to do with relationships with others?

5. "Outrageous scheme"—although not the central point of the story of Ruth, her behavior in lying with Boaz is sometimes hard for us to understand and accept. It raises all kinds of questions for us about morality and sexuality. What is your reaction to this portion of the story? What interpretation do you place upon it? In what ways, if any, does it challenge your own understandings of sexuality and morality? In the story of Ruth, this scene is placed in the context of a desire for divine blessing. Boaz becomes the instrument of God's blessing. In what ways, in contemporary life, do you see sexual behavior and God's blessing linked? What does it mean to be a person of integrity in one's sexual life?

6. "Redeeming the land"—one of the secondary themes of the story of Ruth has to do with stewardship, the land and its productivity, food and famine, and God's relationship to all this. What are the requirements and/or signs of good stewardship in the story? What difference do you identify in the way Boaz and the unnamed kinsman view Naomi's land? Redemption is a common word in Christian theology. In this story, it is applied to the land. What kinds of images does the phrase, "redeeming the land," bring to your mind? What does it seem to mean in this story? What does it mean to be a person of integrity in relation to land, property, and possessions?

7. "Radical faith"—Phyllis Trible describes Ruth as "the model of a radical faith which dares to risk all." How do you react when you hear the phrase "radical faith"? Is it a familiar way for you to talk and think, or does it jar your mind? Why? What does Dr. Trible seem to mean by "radical faith"? Is the faith you have a "radical faith"? What does having a "radical faith" have to do with being a person of integrity?

8. "God's intervention"—where is God in this story of radical faith? Phyllis Trible states that "the human condition itself reveals divine activity." Where do you see divine activity in the story? Where in the human condition today do you see God at work? Where in the everyday events of your own life do you see him at work? In what ways is your experience of God like or unlike that of Ruth and Naomi? How does the God you see at work affect your understanding of what it means to be a person of integrity?

Fred Young pictures Nehemiah as a person concerned about rebuilding the inner city. He offers examples of modern-day Nehemiahs who share that concern, and he calls us to become such persons. This study focuses our attention upon the relationship between the Word of the Lord and the big political, economic, and social issues of our day while underlining the use of practical skills, physical labor, and material resources in his service.

Preparatory Reading: Nehemiah 1:1–2:20
Nehemiah 4:1–5:13
Nehemiah 12:44-47; 13:10-14

Nehemiah, the Builder
by Fred Young

Nehemiah (whose name means "the Lord is compassionate—the Lord comforts") was a Jew whose second home was Susa. His first home was Jerusalem. Susa (in Hebrew *Shushan* or *Susan*) means "lily." Some think that the abundant presence of lilies gave the name to the city. Oleanders, oaks, rich pasturage, and orange and lemon trees characterize the land from December through March.

Considerable ruins at Susa indicate a once great city. These include a pillared hall built on the model of the Hall of Xerxes at Persepolis. Thirty-six of the pillars form a throne room two hundred feet square, the second largest throne room in the ancient world. Only the throne room at Karnak is larger. Esther 1:6 indicates that there were beautiful curtains around the king's audience room. Remains of varicolored slab pavement still show. Jews living there enjoyed relative peace and harmony. The bulk of the population was friendly to the Jews (cf. Esther 3:15; 8:15).

According to the records from ancient Persia, the king's household included secret service agents, secretaries, stewards, chamberlains, cupbearers, musicians, eunuchs for the harem, and stable boys for the king's horses. The table of the king often fed 15,000 persons in a given day. The food was furnished by the provinces. Sheep, goats, wild asses, horses, camels, poultry, and ostriches were consumed. The king usually ate alone. Sometimes the queen, queen mother, brothers, and children ate with the king. It was said that the king drank only Helbon wine, the famous wine from the Helbon Valley north of Damascus.

Nehemiah was the cupbearer of the king. Cupbearers were carefully selected. Looks, temperament, political mood, and other personal characteristics were considered. Cupbearers tasted the wine from the vessel from which the king drank, and they guarded the entrance to the royal harem. Cheerfulness on all occasions was expected of the cupbearer.

One day the king noticed that Nehemiah was not as cheerful as he usually was. Upon inquiring, he found out that Nehemiah's brother, Hanani, had sent word to Nehemiah about the condition of the city of Jerusalem. He said that the situation was extremely bad. People were suffering and the physical situation was in decline. Streets and buildings were in need of repair. The wall was broken at many points and homes were unfit for habitation. When Nehemiah got the report, he broke down and wept. Jerusalem was the home of his family line. He could not bear to see it in this shape.

Nehemiah did something that was not too unusual. He prayed about the matter. His prayer is a model prayer for someone who wants to do something constructive. He asked forgiveness for the deeds done by the people that brought about the sad situation. Then he prayed that God would use him in the process of rebuilding (1:5-11).

Nehemiah could have taken up a collection among his friends and sent it to his brother, Hanani, to be used for the relief of the poor. That would have helped a little—for the time being. He could have proposed that a petition be drawn up for lower taxes or an urban renewal project, signed by many and sent to the proper authorities. He could have called for a prayer meeting and asked for a season of prayer for the poor suffering Jews living in shameful conditions. Instead he asked God to use him in rebuilding the inner city.

The future in the cities of the United States is not bright. Living conditions in the inner city, increasing crime rates and joblessness, and overcrowding and oppression of the poor by the rich paint a gloomy picture. The sad thing is that not many really care about what is going on in the heart of our cities. Most are too busy making a living or enjoying the fruits of good living to tune in on the cries of those suffering in the inner city. Newspaper reports of rape and robbery and TV special reports of conditions in the inner city stir the emotions very slightly. Here and there, thank God, a "Nehemiah" weeps and then prays that God will use him to cleanse and purify the wounded and broken heart of a city.

The king gave Nehemiah permission to go to Jerusalem and survey the damage. He rode on horseback around the city, observing the situation and laying plans for the rebuilding. What he found on his city tour were broken walls, burned-out gates, and ruined areas. The city had not been rebuilt or cleaned up from the attack of Nebuchadnezzar over a century earlier. The sight of the ruins called for concerned citizens to act quickly and promptly. Nehemiah did just this. His response involved some drastic moves from the wealth and splendor of Susa to the needy, depressed areas of Jerusalem.

A modern "Nehemiah" lived and worked in one of our troubled cities. The trustees of the church said to him, "Would you like to live in the suburbs in a fashionable home like ours?" He replied, "No, if I am to be the pastor here, I want to live near the church." No urging on their part would change his mind. It was not easy. On dark nights he would wait for the sound of the engine of the car his wife was driving as she returned from a women's meeting in the nearby community, and he would hurry to turn on the garage lights in the alley so she and he would be safe from would-be attackers. On Wednesday evenings he would walk home with the few who would come to prayer meeting, even though their homes or apartments were only a few blocks away. Knocks at the door and telephone calls late in the night brought messages of distress at all hours. Trips down dark streets and up winding stairs to sick rooms in dimly lit surroundings were common. The city was in a pitiable condition physically and a nearly hopeless situation spiritually. The only way this "Nehemiah" could take it day after day and week after week was through the power of prayer each morning that God would in some way heal broken lives and mend broken hearts and that God would use him in the process.

A little Chinese girl, the product of a sailor and a prostitute, lived in one of the apartments in the inner city. One day "Nehemiah" found her and invited her to a better way of life. After some discussion by the group of deacons, who lived in the suburbs, she was baptized and joined the youth group. She joined the "Order of Nehemiah" and became a builder and brought in some of her friends.

One day a girl with physical handicaps came straggling in. She found in the work of the Lord, through "Nehemiah" and his crew, a place where people did not laugh at handicaps and tattered clothes.

A hardened sailor one day came into the morning worship and sat near the front. It was evident that he had been drinking. During the invitation he came forward. That afternoon, someone from the church called at the second-story apartment where he lived. In a very bare room, he poured out a sad story of sin and brokenness. Someone in the inner city ministered to his needs. Modern "Nehemiahs" care about those who live in broken homes, with broken hearts.

"Nehemiah" need not be male! There are women in our time who are deeply concerned about building better communities. Some women, successful in professional life, visit stores in the inner city to check on prices. They advise the poor when and how to make purchases. They help them to plan budgets. A group of lay persons formed a credit union in the inner city. They taught the members of the credit union how to save and how to spend. A lawyer's wife gave time each week to visiting elderly persons in a depressed area. She took church literature with her on her visits, wrote notes and letters to many of the shut-ins, and learned of needs which were reported to boards of deacons for prompt action. Most of the expense of her work was borne by herself or by her family.

Some jobs can be done at little or no cost. Other jobs require blueprints, surveying, and materials. These necessitate money as well as time. This kind of building means long hours in committee meetings and heavy pledging by the committee members before bringing the proposal to the congregation. It may mean blood, sweat, and tears.

In a large city in the Midwest a group of young women faced certain lives of failure and depression. Some were black; some were white; all were pregnant and halfway through high school. The school authorities required that they discontinue their education. Their outlook on life was dim indeed. A concerned group of citizens looked into their tragic and hopeless situation. These citizens asked a Baptist church if facilities in the church could be used to allow these girls to continue their education. Some Sanballats (see Nehemiah 2:19) objected, but the Nehemiahs won out. Certified teachers volunteered, and girls from the inner city were contacted and urged to enroll. Many did, and one bright day in June the superintendent of schools presented diplomas to a large number of elated young women. The spiritual and moral structure of the inner city was boosted in the process. The materials in this case were human beings; the biblical Nehemiah built anew the city of Jerusalem with stone and mortar. Modern Nehemiahs build the cities with human materials.

Urban renewal may be accomplished in various ways. It may mean old buildings torn down and new streets constructed. It may mean new office buildings and high-rise apartments. It may mean the

building of new spirit and new hope in the lives of persons. Both new buildings and a new spirit can be built. It takes the efforts and means of concerned citizens to accomplish urban renewal in both instances. If we are to adopt an evangelistic life style, we can learn from the approach of Nehemiah. He knew who he was, had compassion in his heart for the needs of his brothers and sisters, made some radical changes in his own life style, and did something that made a difference in the lives of others.

The challenge of Nehemiah to our day is for men and women who live in the better parts of our community to hear the cries of those who live in tragic or unseemly circumstances. The challenge involves taking a look—in a church survey of an area or in a private tour on one's own. Nehemiah inspected the city of Jerusalem on his own. He was not a member of a visitation committee or of an appointed group. He simply wanted to see it on his own.

Most of us love to visit the beauty spots in our land. The lakes, parks, and scenic spots attract us on weekends and on vacation. Sometime take a weekend or part of a vacation and look over the part of the community which you usually avoid. If it is dangerous, take someone with you or go in daylight. Meet some of the people who live there and find out about their crushed hopes and bruised spirits. Listen to their stories of low income and high costs of living. Listen to them tell about their inability to provide a decent education for their children, let alone provide proper dental and medical care for the family. Look at the aging structures, unpainted walls, and high fences. As you visit with them, think about what it would take to build new hopes and ideals in the persons you are visiting. You and I can be modern Nehemiahs—builders of the Spirit.

Nehemiah gave out of his own pocket toward the project of rebuilding. Many can survey a situation and assess the cost needed to make it a better situation. Many have the ability to raise funds for worthy causes. They can lay need upon the hearts of others in such a way that money comes pouring in like corn in an elevator chute. This is good and is often most helpful. Nehemiah did it in a different way. He gave generously of his *own* resources and called upon others to help in the work. You and I can give of what we have.

It is always easier to raise money than it is to give it. It is always easier to make the announcement that workers are needed than it is to put on the overalls and start to work. God wants us to do something about what we know and to give of ourselves in the doing.

The Hebrew word *dabar* means "words" and "deeds." This biblical idea, reflected throughout the story of Nehemiah, relates "speaking" and "doing." This is also true in another way, in the Genesis account of creation. God spoke and it was done. In yet another way Ezekiel heard the Word of the Lord, and then he did some symbolic act that illustrated the content of the message. What I am getting at is, when the inner city cries out, we need to respond in active and constructive ways.

Nehemiah was also concerned about the effect of the financial situation on those who ministered to the physical and religious needs of the poor. Levites, men of God, had to leave their sacred duties because they were not paid living wages. The tithes of the Hebrews were to be given to the Levites. They had no inheritance in Israel as did the other Israelites. Most of the Old Testament links the Levites with the poor and the widows, indicating the poverty of the Levites.

In most denominations a number of pastors are on salary support. Some are on less than the minimum set by their denomination. Some Nehemiahs a few years ago called this to the attention of their national leaders and their ministers. There followed a program that gave new hope and courage to men and women serving in small congregations.

Businessmen with business acumen, C.P.A.'s and others could be Nehemiahs building solid economic structures to support our religious leadership in the cities. Many good ministers do not want to

leave downtown churches any more than rural ministers want to leave country churches. They do leave because they simply cannot find enough money to lead decent lives and pay the normal costs of living. What is needed is to find some Nehemiahs, who care, to build economic supports for the modern "Levites."

Nehemiah was a builder. He knew how to use the square and compass. He knew the use of the trowel and mortarboard. He also knew how to build character and loyalty. Both mechanical and interpersonal skills are needed in our cities today.

We see physically run-down areas in many of our cities, and we observe spiritual need on every side street. We need builders who know how to assess the cost and then know how to gather together others in the rebuilding process. Our Jerusalems are in every state. The Nehemiahs come from laity and clergy. The age of our Nehemiahs varies from teenager to grandma and grandpa. Nehemiah practiced a very practical faith. He did what needed to be done at the time. He was not bothered by the taunts and jeers of others—nor was he slowed down by their threats. He kept alert to every situation and just kept on rebuilding.

Our day is becoming more and more influenced by the philosophy and theology of the end. Some would despair of the future and would advise no action. These gloom spreaders include ecologists, playwrights, economists, and theologians. They claim we have so polluted the air and streams, used up the natural resources, degraded the mind and soul, and offended the grace of God that only gloom and darkness lie ahead.

The Lord will come as he has promised. He will come in the time appointed. Our work is to be busy doing his will in the community of men and women. Cities need to be rebuilt. Streets and parks must be constructed. Run-down areas need to be renewed. This will happen where Nehemiahs survey the area, get off their horses, and take up the spade and pick. Brokenness in human lives, economic injustices, poor schools for potentially creative youth and adults, and spiritual deprivation must be recognized. Spiritual renewal will take place when the Nehemiahs of our time dig into their pockets and help pay the cost of the rebuilding of the spirit of men and women.

Nehemiah had a lot going for himself. He could have kept it that way. He did not. He loved the city which gave birth to his great nation. He wanted to see it renewed physically, socially, and spiritually. He could not do all of it by himself. He did what he could do best. He gave himself and he gave of himself. Then others were recruited and the job was accomplished.

Let us look at our own situation. Then let us look at the condition of our cities and become builders. How can we do less than Nehemiah?

SHARING OUR INSIGHTS

Our skills as persons vary. Some of us work well with our hands. Others are better in the area of human relationships. Some are artists and some are scientists. Some excel at cooking meals. Nehemiah seems to have been a man with a very practical bent. He took the skills he had and put them to work. He challenges us to become builders. This study suggests several elements that went into his work as a builder. Discussing some of them may help us clarify what we have to offer and how we might become builders.

1. "A model prayer"—Fred Young says that Nehemiah's prayer, found in chapter 1, verses 5-11, is "a model prayer for someone who wants to do something constructive." Becoming a builder seems to begin with prayer, seemingly a very impractical approach. How do you respond to that insight? Is prayer part of the preparation you see as important before you act to rebuild society? The prayer begins with repentance. What kind of repenting do we need to do today if we are to be effective

builders in relation to the crises of our day? What does prayer have to do with integrity?

2. "Not many really care"—Fred Young states "that not many really care about what is going on in the heart of our cities." Do you agree? What does it mean to care? What did it mean for Nehemiah? Why is it important to care? What does caring about the inner city have to do with integrity? Do you care?

3. "Inspected the city"—Nehemiah looked around the city to examine the damage. Fred Young suggests that we might visit the inner city instead of going to our usual recreational spots. Have you ever visited communities or parts of the city where poverty prevailed? Have you ever talked with any of the people who lived there? The first step in becoming a builder is finding out what the situation is and how people feel about it. What are ways in which you might "inspect the city"? Perhaps you live in the inner city. If so, how do you feel about Fred Young's proposal? What is it that you want people to know about the inner city? How can we learn how to talk and become builders together?

4. "Some drastic moves"—Nehemiah made "some drastic moves from the wealth and splendor of Susa to the needy, depressed areas of Jerusalem." Becoming a builder, for him, was a drastic move. Is there a considerable gap between your life style and that of people in needy, depressed areas? What would it mean for you to make a drastic move? For Nehemiah, it meant actually moving into the inner city. Is that what it means for everyone? Are there perhaps needy and depressed areas where you live? Maybe you already live in the inner city or in a rural depressed area. How would you interpret the story of Nehemiah? What is its message for you, and what do you think it says to suburbanites? What does it say about integrity as a part of the Christian life style?

5. "Mechanical and interpersonal skills"—Fred Young calls us to "give of what we have . . . to give of ourselves in the doing." We are to use the skills we have. What skills do you have that could be used to rebuild society? Do you have mechanical skills? Are you good with people? What are the skills you use to earn a living? How could you use those skills to become a modern Nehemiah—as a volunteer, through your job, through a change in your life style? What does it mean to treat our skills with integrity?

6. "The building of new spirit"—at the heart of Nehemiah's

building program is the call to "remember the Lord" (Nehemiah 4:14). Fred Young talks about the "building of new spirit and new hope in the lives of people." Why should we even be interested in rebuilding the city? What hope is there? What is the basis of your hope? How would you go about helping others see that hope? How does one go about building a new spirit? What kind of spirit is needed? What would it mean for you to be a builder of a new spirit? Why is a new spirit important and what does it have to do with being a person of integrity? What resources of the spirit already exist among people in depressed areas?

F. Lenore Kruse tells us a story in this chapter about Peter, linking together some typical incidents in his life. Within the scope of a few pages, what more can one do but touch the highlights of so complex a personality? Miss Kruse acquaints us with the heights and depths of his moods, starkly seen as strengths and weaknesses which lie within each of us. But the story she tells is more than a biography. It is a theological statement, reflecting her own bent toward theology. The events of Peter's life illumine the meaning of wholeness as a gift of grace.

Preparatory Reading: Luke 5:1-11
Mark 8:27–9:13
Matthew 14:22-33
Matthew 26:31-75
John 21:15-19
Acts 1:12-26
Acts 2:14-42
Acts 10:1-48

Peter's Moods on the Road to Wholeness
by F. Lenore Kruse

Peter was quick. What he felt, he expressed. Words rarely failed him, and to become leader and spokesman for the Twelve was as natural as breathing. It does not follow that he was any more whole than the others. Wholeness is not a "born" characteristic, known only by persons of a particular disposition. It was, for him as for all, his Lord's gift to him. Peter's responsibility was the task of taking that gift of wholeness into his thoughts and feelings, into the events of his life. At the same time, the kind of person Peter was brings his struggles home to us with such vivid force that we find ourselves identifying with him and making him *our* spokesman, too!

Peter's presence is so strong in the Gospel stories that one can hardly get a picture of the man without reading all four Gospels, the first twelve chapters of The Acts of the Apostles, and Peter's own letter to Christian communities in Asia Minor. It would be rewarding to do so. This study, however, will focus on only a few events typical of his struggle to make that gift the consistent operating center of his life and being.

Peter's Call (Luke 5:1-11)

We have a tendency, from reading the accounts as they are placed in Matthew (4:12-25) and Mark (1:14-39), to think of Jesus' call to Peter and his fisher-companions as coming to them virtually "out of the blue." John's Gospel, however (1:35-42), suggests that Andrew and Peter, at least, had taken time off from their family business to join the crowds heading for the lower Jordan to listen to the preacher who was creating such a stir. Something more than just the daily business of earning a living and maintaining a home must therefore have already been knocking at the door of their spirits. The writer of that Gospel states that Andrew had even become a disciple of John the Baptist. When Jesus was pointed out to him, he not only followed after him, but he also brought his brother Simon to him. It could have been there that Jesus first knew Peter and recognized the potential which called forth the nickname "Peter," the Rock.

Jesus, however, had not yet chosen *them*. It was back to their fishing business. When Jesus returned to Galilee, he taught in their synagogues, preaching and engaging in such amazing action that the whole countryside was stirred up. Luke describes a whole series of such events and pronouncements (4:14-44) before he records the calling of any disciples, leaving no room for anyone to question that Jesus stood for anything less than a whole new way of understanding life and living in society. To make a positive response to his message would mean accepting change. And change always comes hard. Jesus was making sure that anyone whom he called would know pretty well what he was letting himself in for.

Peter was hearing all this. He was absorbing the news and the flying rumors with which all Capernaum was buzzing. And he had the episode on the banks of the Jordan to remember. Jesus had even visited him since then and had brought healing to his own sick mother-in-law. It is amazing, however, how we can respond to something we have heard but which has not yet touched the core of our own inner being.

Then all of a sudden it was happening to Peter himself. It was *his* boat into which Jesus stepped, asking him to shove off a bit so he could speak to the crowds. It was Peter himself who must listen with

Jesus right beside him. It was *his* nets which Jesus told him to let down for a catch. Peter had respect; he would not refuse, even though he doubted anything could happen since they had already tried without success. But when the miracle really did happen, and to *him,* he thought, "Oh, no, no! If it's *me* you mean, I don't want it that close! I'm not good enough. It all sounds wonderful, and I approve. But let me be! I haven't got what you say it takes! You need somebody better than me! Please go away!" Jesus addressed the panic which surged through Peter, tearing him apart: *"Do not be afraid.* From now on you will catch men." Luke tells us nothing more—except that as soon as they could bring home their overloaded boats, Peter and his companions left everything, to follow him. Jesus was not looking for the perfect person—the wholly adequate person. He was calling Peter in full knowledge of exactly who and what Peter was: sinful, mixed in his weaknesses and strengths, capable of both much good and much evil.

It happens. Circumstances bring about a decisive moment. Assurance enters from beyond. In its support a decision is made with the swiftness of a plunging eagle, fear swept away as if it had never been there. Jesus moved in to create the circumstances which brought it about for Peter. His living Spirit is present, ready to move in upon us now.

Even so, Peter's calling was not yet "sealed and delivered." Jesus gave them all a long and close taste of what they might expect (Luke 5:29–6:11). He invited other disciples. Undoubtedly there were others as well who attached themselves out of their own desire. But finally a day came when Jesus went into the hills to pray. He had given them time to be sure of their decisions, and Jesus himself had had time to observe and check his first impressions. Now he laid out before God all of his thinking, continuing through the night in prayer. "When it was day, he called his disciples, and chose from them twelve . . ." (Luke 6:13). These would be his apostles-in-training, who would share in his mission without further reservation. And "Simon, whom he named Peter," headed the list (6:14).

A Lesson About Power (Matthew 14:22-33)

On this occasion, the disciples were helpless against a storm which struck them as they rowed across the lake. Their fear and distress got through to Jesus at his place of prayer, but it was heightened by his appearance on the water. Peter's part in this story, however, arouses in us the feeling of embarrassment we experience when someone we usually think highly of is guilty of some speech or action which seems neither to fit the person's position nor the occasion.

Peter's response seems strongly like that of another Simon he was to meet in the future. That other Simon "was carried away when he saw the powerful signs and miracles that were taking place" (Acts 8:13, NEB). Coveting the power for himself as an end in itself, he tried to buy it from Peter (Acts 8:18-19). Perhaps it was the outcome of this experience which enabled Peter, when that time came, to respond as he did to that other Simon in Samaria (Acts 20:24).

Jesus accepted Peter in love, on the level where Peter was revealing himself to be. He did not even rebuke the brashness which drove Peter to demand that Jesus give proof of himself beyond the words, "It is I" (Matthew 14:27). He simply responded, "Come." Peter was caught in his own low motives, for only singleness of heart in allegiance to God's own uses of power, reflecting some quality of Jesus' own reason for having come, could have held back the fear which seized him as the gale hit him full force. A desire to allay the terror the other disciples felt—a need to recover his own courage by moving as close to Jesus as possible—would have stood between him and his demoralizing fear.

What a blow Jesus dealt the "eye for an eye" principle which is so frequently championed to this very day! Legalistic justice would have allowed Peter to experience the full consequences of his misdirected reach for personal power and glory. But in his own understanding of justice as redemptive and merciful, Jesus met Peter's cry, "Save me, Lord!" with the strong grasp which pulled him to safety. His only rebuke was, "Why did you hesitate? How little faith you have!" (Matthew 14:31, NEB).

Only Matthew records this incident. But as a demonstration of where our Lord stands with the person who is losing his battle to enter fully into his Lord's gift of wholeness—integrity—this event has no equal.

Christians will inevitably differ in the ways they understand and deal with miracles recorded in the Gospels. Nevertheless, miracle as an event which defies normal explanation is the only way to make sense out of the freedom we know—the freedom from having to earn the approval of God by our righteousness. A life of integrity is an expression of our gratitude for the miracle of freedom in Christ to be who we were created to be and his affirmation of us even when we fall short of that intended wholeness.

Confession and Denial (Mark 8:27–9:13; Matthew 26:31-75)

As one follows the experiences of Peter through these passages, his stand-out qualities, his leadership, and his uniqueness are not the things which come through most clearly, but his likeness to so many human beings. He was only more, not different, at the core. He did not distinguish himself by his conduct. He was always the first to see, the first to act. What he did was shameful, too, and more so. Suddenly Peter begins to fade in one's consciousness and Jesus' response to Peter fills the space. The incident in the water becomes the prototype for all that followed—Jesus grasping the sinking Peter's hand in answer to his panicked cry, "Save me, Lord!" Having reached out and caught hold of him, they *both* climbed into the boat. Without Jesus, Peter's special abilities and insights had little point, except to give him less excuse for his failures. But Jesus knew full well that the possession of superior ability does not insure wholeness. It only makes the crash of one's fallings louder. Jesus knew this about Peter and gave him time. Peter babbled during that supreme moment on the mountaintop (Mark 9:5) and Jesus let it pass. He sorrowed but accepted Peter's inability to stay awake to share his own agonized vigil in the Garden. He undid the damage of Peter's flailing sword when the rabble came. He reached him with a look of utter compassion for his denial during the trial. It was only when Peter tried directly to interfere with his own interpretation of his mission that he sternly rebuked Peter. And he seized with joy that swift confession, "You are the Messiah," using it as a milestone in his own journey. Wholeness—integrity—was a gift he had given, not a prior possession of Peter. He would trust Peter and support him in the slow and often painful process of growing in it and making it a living reality in his actions.

That conversation in Caesarea Philippi was important to Jesus in his relationship with his disciples and to his own mission. It revealed that Peter really had been making progress in understanding that gift of wholeness. Jesus had not voiced messianic claims for himself. He had even always silenced those who tried to express it—until now. So Peter's forthright answer to his question "Who do you say I am?" must have been a real validation of his faith in Peter—helping to hold it firm all through the terrible revelations to come—of how long a way he still had to go in his struggle for the integrity which lay as a gift in his hands, so hard to take and use. It was of a piece with Peter's always coming back to try again. Peter knew the gift was given, and no collapse could end wholly in despair. Always he had the remembrance of that undeserved response to his cry, "Lord, save me!"

Twice particularly Jesus had made it clear what wholeness involved. We often assume that the Sermon on the Mount was preached to the crowds. "When he saw the crowds he went up the hill" (Matthew 5:1, NEB). But the story continues, "There he took his seat, and when his *disciples* had gathered around he began to address them" (italics added). But on that eventful day in Caesarea Philippi, with his mission in the world once and for all established with his own disciples, he broadened his audience to include all within hearing to say, "Anyone who wishes to be a follower of mine must leave self behind; he must take up his cross, and come with me. . . . What does a man gain by winning the whole world at the cost of his true self?" (Mark 8:34-37, NEB). And Peter struggled on.

Feed My Sheep (John 21:15-19)

Who has not bled with Peter, having to live with himself and the echo of those words spoken in the court beside the fire as Jesus was being tried: "I do not know this man you speak of"? But his tears tell us much. There is healing in tears. God be praised that we are beginning to admit that tears belong to men as well as women. That Peter wept tells us he had begun to use Jesus' gift of wholeness more fully than the act of denial showed. His tears expressed rejection of his own base act.

Jesus' look must have conveyed to Peter assurance that the gift of wholeness was still his, that Jesus would never withdraw it. There was room for recovery, impossible though it seemed at the moment. So it is not really surprising that Peter was there with the others to receive the news of the empty tomb, even though in the angel's message to the wondering women Peter's name no longer came first. In later testimony (1 Corinthians 15:5, Luke 24:34), Jesus was even reported to have appeared first to Simon among the eleven.

Peter was still Peter. When Jesus was seen on the shore in the early morning, Peter impulsively jumped overboard in his eagerness to get to him. This did not mean that all was as before. The fact of Peter's denial still lay between them, in need of being confessed before forgiveness could be complete. Jesus opened the conversation, in words which carried much freight. Peter, having demonstrated to the full the human capacity for baseness, found it was not greater than his Lord's capacity for forgiveness. In response to Jesus' question, "Do you love me?" he said, "Lord, *you know* I love you!" To say that, under the circumstances, was as great a statement of faith as his declaration on the way to Caesarea, "You are the Messiah." What a far distance he had come from that day of his first calling when he tried to push Jesus out of his life rather than risk what it might do to him! And what a distance from the moment in that other boat when he tried to make himself equal to his Master in a display of superhuman power! Broken apart? No. Whole? Yes—not by his own achievement, but by the grace of Christ coupled to his own capacity for response in repentance.

The conversation with Peter on the lakeside was not only an occasion for forgiveness and restoration of his discipleship, but it was also a kind of graduation into the apostleship for which he had been in training. When Jesus said, "Feed my lambs; tend my sheep; feed my sheep," he was communicating to Peter that love is not only feeling. It is action. Jesus was telling Peter what love entailed. Here was Peter's commission: "Feed my sheep." As a disciple he could focus on Jesus, although even there he had to learn by doing, by sharing in the work of his Master. As an apostle his focus would be on the field of mission, but it would be in a rhythm of responsible service alternating with return for renewal of strength and spirit in worship, rest, and "continuing education."

For his mission as an apostle Peter had the pattern of Jesus' own ministry to go by. He had seen how Jesus "went about . . . teaching in their synagogues and preaching the gospel of the kingdom and healing every disease and every infirmity among the people" (Matthew 4:23). Those infirmities, Peter had seen, were of both body and spirit, and of both separate persons and institutions (witness Jesus' confrontation with Judaism itself, in cleansing the temple, in breaking ceremonial laws which were stifling the people, and in free association with despised groups—Samaritans, publicans). But Peter would need to go beyond imitating Jesus' own ministry. Greater things than these shall you do, his Master had said (see John 14:12); and "I have other sheep, that are not of this fold; I must bring them also" (John 10:16). No rigid pattern would be set for Peter to follow. Whatever tending was called for, whatever might be implied in any particular time or place in the command to feed his sheep, wherever the lambs were folded, wherever the sheep might stray—that was what an apostle of Jesus Christ was commissioned to do; that was where his apostle was commissioned to be—whether Peter, or you, or me. "To love me is to tend and feed my lambs and sheep."

Peter's Ministry (Acts 1–4)

The early chapters of Acts show us Peter acting in his characteristic way from the outset, taking the lead in the small community of faith. Now as never before, his experience of the wholeness which had been given, confirmed, and renewed by his Lord was tested. It held, making him bold in witnessing to Christ's resurrection in the hostile world outside his supporting community as well as exercising leadership within it.

Power had been given him and the other apostles, beyond anything they had ever known, as their Lord had promised them. They had been told to wait in Jerusalem for this gift of the Holy Spirit which would come upon them. They had lived through the testing of ten

days of waiting in prayer. Prayer within the community of believers as days of waiting before God, being open to him in expectancy, is rarely practiced now, even though the desire for a new visitation of the Spirit in all its ancient power is often expressed. Perhaps there is no way today for the Christian community or any part of it to do this—or bring itself to believe it is necessary. Nevertheless, in our present age the relation of the church to the rest of the world is more like that of these first days than in the days when Christianity was the unquestioned basis for all of Western society. It is no longer dominant as an institution, or much heeded in the circles of science and technology which have become the dominant forces and which have so greatly changed the framework of our existence. We may therefore need to find and do that which for our day is comparable to that long period of waiting in prayer if we are to be as effectual in witness now as were they.

Just as it was with Jesus, preaching was the first vehicle through which this small band of Spirit-filled persons began their mission, with Peter still their spokesman. Jesus' message was, "Repent, for the kingdom of God is at hand." His proclamation was that Isaiah's promise of good news for the poor, release for the captives, recovery of sight for the blind, liberty for the oppressed, and the arrival of "the acceptable year of the Lord" was being fulfilled. Therefore, repent, and believe the gospel! Peter's message was that of witness to the resurrection of this same Jesus, and his living presence among them as their risen Lord, whom the authorities had crucified so as to suppress that proclamation. This was laying their lives on the line— but Peter did not only confront the authorities with the enormity of what they had done, but also he preached with deep and wonderful persuasion to all who heard: "Repent, and be baptized every one of you in the name of Jesus Christ for the forgiveness of your sins; and you shall receive the gift of the Holy Spirit. For the promise is to you and to your children and to all that are far off, every one whom the Lord our God calls to him" (Acts 2:38-39). They were persuaded— three thousand and more. "And they devoted themselves to the apostles' teaching and fellowship, to the breaking of bread and the prayers" (Acts 2:42). Preaching can be empty sound if the Spirit is absent. But preaching which is the Spirit speaking through the human voice is irresistible, and it is as essential for communication of the gospel today as it was then. Where a church is committed to an evangelistic life style, the Spirit will find those through whom the preached word will come alive and irresistibly evoke the question, "Brethren, what shall we do?"

For all his power in preaching, Peter did not forget the wholeness of the ministry in which he had shared in his days of training with Jesus. He gave himself freely to human need and found the Spirit giving him power to heal as well as to preach. And as he disturbed the ecclesiastical authorities more and more, he learned also to endure suffering for the sake of his Lord, a condition which Jesus had included in that "commissioning" in the early morning encounter beside the sea, knowing that Peter would now be able.

In the community to which we belong, we take that place for which our gifts particularly prepare us. But we keep that place only by acting with an integrity which is born out of a discovery of wholeness in experience and knowledge of both weaknesses and strengths in our own inner being. All that had gone before in Peter's apprenticeship had moved him to such a point; and as the church was born, he fulfilled his leadership in it with a power that demonstrated how fully he had internalized the gift of wholeness he had received from his Lord.

Previously we found our attention on Peter and his struggle for integrity shifting to Jesus and his support of Peter in that struggle. In this phase of Peter's life our attention begins to shift from Peter alone to Peter as one of the Christian community whose life must develop its corporate integrity. There is constant interaction and correction between the community of faith and its separate members. In his continuing freedom to choose, always a part of the maturing human being, Peter remained vulnerable to sinful choice as well as capable of good. So a time came when he needed the support of the Christian community, as once he had needed the support of his Master in the flesh, to keep his integrity and his wholeness alive. This we will note in one final incident in Peter's experience.

Peter in the Gentile World (Acts, chapter 10)

The significance of the Way for the whole world grew slowly in the ministry of the apostles, but it was hastened by persecution which scattered Christian Jews out of Jerusalem into neighboring areas. Peter himself turned over leadership of the Jerusalem community to James and went about ministering to the scattered and growing communities of Christians, who as yet were always believers within Judaism. Then came the incident of the Roman, Cornelius. His interest in and longing for life under the kind of God he saw in the Jewish faith was answered in a dream. He was commanded to go and bring Peter from Joppa to hear a message by which his need would be filled. Meantime, God was preparing Peter for this which would be an unheard-of encounter. The result is described in Acts 10:44-48. News of it reaching the church in Jerusalem created upset, especially through the protest of a party who held strictly to the idea that the Way was a movement purely within Judaism, for Jews only or for full proselytes to the Jewish faith. But Peter, called in to give account of himself, reported the action of God in pouring out his Spirit upon Cornelius and his family. It underscored the conclusion which Peter had reached out of the vision God had sent him as he rested on Simon the Tanner's rooftop and which had resulted in his saying to Cornelius's household, "Truly I perceive that God shows no partiality, but in every nation any one who fears him and does what is right is acceptable to him" (Acts 10:34). This was hard teaching for the Jews who had for so long believed they enjoyed God's special favor, forgetting that he had called them to be his people in order that through them all the families of the earth were to be blessed (Genesis 12:2-3). Is it equally hard teaching for the Christian church today? To move into an evangelistic life style means to recover this under-standing of God, having done with our preoccupation with our life within the institution, and making the Evangel the center of our reason for being.

Peter convinced the Jerusalem church of the rightness of his action in not withholding baptism from Cornelius and his family, and they rejoiced with him. But there were powerful minorities developing where, as now, a particular interpretation was becoming more important than the living Spirit as the basis for unity in the church. As time went on, this tension opened for Peter a whole new "can of worms" which brought his integrity severely to the test. Gentiles were being recognized as legitimate members of the Christian community without first becoming Jews. At the same time the Christian Way was becoming established as an institution. The inevitable differences of opinion and interpretation among influential persons led to parties and factions. All the ceremonial distinctions by which Jews had held Gentiles away from them socially were involved. Evidently Peter found himself shifting back and forth in an attempt to stay in everyone's good graces, until he had to be confronted by Paul with the effect that this was having not only on his own integrity but also on that of others. Paul pointed this out in a letter to the Galatians: "But when Cephas came to Antioch, I opposed him to his face, because he was clearly in the wrong. For until certain persons came from James he was taking his meals with gentile Christians; but when they came he drew back and began to hold aloof, because he was afraid of the advocates of circumcision. The other Jewish Christians showed the same lack of principle; even Barnabas was carried away and played false like the rest" (Galatians 2:11-13, NEB). Peter could be grateful for the ministry of the church to him in helping him recover his integrity.

Conclusion

It can be noted that in every crisis of integrity which Peter faced, a dominant ingredient was fear: fear of inadequacy—fear for his life—fear of disapproval. How well we know the kind of fear that paralyzes and threatens to destroy us! Jesus did not regard it lightly. He moved in to communicate affirming support more sure and more strong than the threat, literally casting out the fear. It is the entrance of his Spirit into ours that insures our wholeness—never perfect, never complete in this life, but never without grace for renewal and movement toward completion.

Remembering what he was as a young disciple, Peter's letter (First Peter) is one of the beautiful evidences of the possibility for growth in wholeness and integrity when one's life is invaded by the Spirit of God. Archibald Hunter says of that letter, "No one can fail to hear the note of courage that rings through it: courage in the teeth of trial and suffering. . . . Nor can anyone miss the pilgrim note. . . . Yet the dominant theme is . . . hope, hope that rests not on man but on God, the living God who is known by his mighty acts . . . and who holds out to the faithful pilgrim at his journey's ending the promise of an inheritance incorruptible and undefiled and that fadeth not away." [1]

"Therefore gird up your minds," says Peter, ". . . set your hope fully upon the grace that is coming to you at the revelation of Jesus Christ. . . . Through him you have confidence in God, who raised him from the dead and gave him glory, so that your faith and hope are in God.

"You are a chosen race, a royal priesthood, a holy nation, God's own people, that you may declare the wonderful deeds of him who called you out of darkness into his marvelous light.

"Have no fear . . . nor be troubled, but in your hearts reverence Christ as Lord.

". . . and after you have suffered . . . the God of all grace, who has called you to his eternal glory in Christ, will himself restore, establish, and strengthen you."   (1 Peter 1:13, 21; 2:9; 3:14*b*-15; 5:10)

[1] *The Interpreter's Bible* (Nashville: Abingdon Press, 1957), vol. 12, p. 77.

SHARING OUR INSIGHTS

The story of Peter, as told us by F. Lenore Kruse, raises questions for us about the place of fear, weakness, ability, and impulse in the life of a Christian. We are forced to struggle with our understanding of the gracious action of God and our incomplete expression of the wholeness which we have received. Growth becomes a key to understanding the meaning of integrity in an evangelistic life style. As we seek to grow further in that life, we may wish to examine the implications of one or more of the following phrases:

1. "A decisive moment"—Lenore Kruse suggests that the story of Peter's life seems to be one of impulsive response at decisive moments. At the same time, she stresses that Jesus wanted his followers to have some idea of what they were letting themselves in for. What have been the decisive moments in your life to which you responded? Did you know what you were letting yourself in for? One of the decisive moments in Peter's life came when he attempted to walk on the water. Miss Kruse notes that in future times of weakness he had the remembrance of that undeserved response to his cry, "Lord, save me!" to sustain him. Do you have similar moments to look back to? How does remembering decisive moments in the past help you to move into the future?

2. "Low motives"—Lenore Kruse compares Peter's behavior during the storm with someone who embarrasses us with "some speech or action which seems neither to fit the person's position nor the occasion." Everyone is frightened. Peter ignores their need and gets carried away with the possibility of walking on water. Can you think of instances where persons or groups have used a disastrous occasion for personal advantage? What happened to Peter in this situation? Why? What did he learn about integrity and wholeness that has meaning for you today?

3. "He was only more"—Lenore Kruse stresses Peter's likeness to so many human beings, except that he reached greater depths and heights. In those extremes he makes more vivid what is in all of us. What does it mean to have shifting moods as a Christian? What did it mean for Peter? Miss Kruse underlines the fact that one's strengths do not necessarily insure wholeness. What does it mean to take our strengths and weaknesses seriously as persons of integrity?

4. "A new visitation of the Spirit"—in the first chapter of Acts, the disciples wait in prayer. Lenore Kruse suggests we may need to

do something comparable, for our day, to that period of waiting in prayer. What does it mean to wait in prayer? When is it appropriate to wait in prayer, and when is the time to move out in action? What does waiting in prayer have to do with integrity?

5. "The support of the Christian community"—Lenore Kruse talks about the corrective interaction between Peter and the Christian community. Sometimes, as a church, we need to be open to what God may be saying to us through even one other person in our midst. Do you experience the church as a supporting community? How can we be a supporting community to one another when we do not all see things in the same way? What does it mean to have integrity as a Christian congregation?

6. "Stay in everyone's good graces"—Peter tried to please everyone in the controversy about Gentile Christians. He seemed to be afraid of what people were going to think of him. Have you ever worried about what people were going to think? Is it possible to be a person of integrity and please everyone?

7. "No partiality"—who are the Gentiles in today's world? Who are the people we try to exclude or make conform? How do we go about being persons of integrity in our relationships with the "Gentiles" of today?

8. "Feed my sheep"—Lenore Kruse uses this passage to illustrate both the nature of Peter's wholeness and a new depth in his mission. What is involved in Peter's telling Jesus he loves him? Do you ever tell him of your love? What was Jesus saying about Peter's love when he responded, "Feed my sheep"? What might it mean for you to feed his sheep? What does this brief encounter tell us about our wholeness, our integrity, and our mission?

9. "The miracle of freedom"—Lenore Kruse talks about a life of integrity as one in which we are thankful for the freedom to express ourselves and receive "his affirmation . . . even when we fall short. . . ." Do you ever feel yourself in the tension between what you could be, what God says you can be, and the way you actually behave? If wholeness is a gift, how do we take growing seriously? Where do you see both gift and growth in your own life?

Fred Young pictures Jonathan as a person of daring, a friend, and one who was willing to let someone else take first place. He tells us the story of the effect of the decisiveness of one person. Jonathan decided and acted, and it made a difference. Fred Young illustrates the power of some modern Jonathans and suggests some ways in which we might move from these models to an evangelistic life style of our own.

Preparatory Reading: 1 Samuel, chapters 13-14; 19-20

Jonathan, Daring Leader and Humble Friend
by Fred Young

Jonathan's Background

Jonathan, whose name means "the Lord has given," was the eldest son of King Saul. Jonathan's home was just a few miles north of Jerusalem in the rolling hills that formed part of the central ridge in Palestine. Archaeologists have found the ruins of the home of King Saul, the place from which he governed Israel. Jonathan grew up in this spacious house.

Our first knowledge of Jonathan comes from a military engagement between the Philistines and the Israelites. These two foes were long-term enemies, both attempting to take over the land of Canaan. The Philistines occupied the rich farmlands by the sea, in the Pentapolis (five-city league), while the Israelites occupied the high ridge that cut through Canaan. At this particular time in Israelite history the Philistines were moving out of the farmlands and were threatening the hill country around Bethel. They sought to control the caravan route that led north from Jerusalem through the Shechem Pass into the Megiddo Valley and on toward Damascus.

The Philistines made life miserable for the Israelites. Raiding parties looted cities and countryside. To make matters worse, the Philistines gained control of all the military weapons. They forbade all blacksmithing, which meant that the Israelites could not forge weapons. Only agricultural implements were allowed, and even these could be repaired only in Philistine blacksmith shops. Saul and Jonathan were the only ones who possessed sword and spear.

The Philistines greatly outnumbered the Israelites. There were so many Philistines that the author of 1 Samuel 13 says they were like the sand on the seashore. They came in thousands of chariots with hundreds of cavalrymen. The Israelites came with broomsticks and slingshots!

Two thousand of the Israelite army were stationed with Saul at Michmash and in the surrounding hills near Bethel; the remaining soldiery were quartered at Geba in the tribal territory of Benjamin. These were under the command of Saul's son, Jonathan.

In an initial skirmish, Jonathan's men bested the defenses of the Philistines stationed near their camp at Geba. Exactly what happened is not clear. Apparently an outpost was overrun. This defeat angered the Philistines, and they massed at Michmash to challenge the tiny army of Saul. The size of the Philistine forces struck terror into the heart of Saul's army. It so frightened the Israelites that out of the combined forces of Saul and Jonathan only six hundred remained in their places. The rest fled westward into the Transjordan area. Saul and Jonathan tried to regroup near Gilgal.

Looking the Situation Over (1 Samuel 14:1-52)

The situation was desperate indeed. Jonathan was acutely aware of this and made some daring moves. He did not call a meeting of the military strategy committee, nor did he seek the advice of the general. He simply picked up his armor and asked his armor bearer to go with him on a very dangerous mission. The armor bearer was most willing, and together they approached the enemy.

Speed has always been an effective weapon in fighting. A boxer with a lightning left jab, a runner with a sudden burst of speed, and an athletic team that can score first often spell the difference between success and defeat. Readiness to move quickly is the essential element in securing the victory.

The account of what took place (1 Samuel 14) indicates that Jonathan had instant success in the ensuing fight and that the Philistine troops then panicked. The account also indicates that the earth quaked, adding to the panic. This has always been the story of biblical faith. Numbers counted little in the decisive battles fought in Israel. Numbers counted little in the early victories of the church from the days of the twelve disciples to the days of the apostles and the early church.

What really counted in Jonathan's case was his courage to do something as one individual and to do it promptly. He knew he was a king's son. He knew he was a commander of men. He also knew he had a sword and a spear. He had authority and he had resources. He was also acutely aware of the power of the enemy. With all this in mind he used everything he had in a daring and brave manner. One man, with some courage and speed, can start almost anything!

If Jonathan had waited until more recruits had been called, or until better weapons could be secured, the day would have been lost. If we wait until the enemy is matched in numbers and in technology, the battle may never be waged and the victory never won. We must use what we have at hand. God said to Moses, "What is that in your hand?" Moses responded, "A rod" (Exodus 4:2); and God used this through Moses. So will He use what we have when we give it to him. This does not negate the need for planning and preparing. It does suggest that in some situations speed and courage are most essential.

Some men know all that they have is "nine hours of college and a few years of faithful pastoring." They do not complain about lack of preparation and resources. One man such as these gave what he had, and a two-parish field won a great victory for God, changing lives of young and old.

So many things we say we will do for God are put off until the time

is ripe, the resources plentiful, and the strategy in perfect form. While these things are in process, the enemy masses and pillages the land.

There are some people who function best by making daring moves. If they think it over, they know they will never make the move. They act quickly with what they have, and amazing things happen. Sometimes it has to do with money. They have some—not much— but like Jonathan's usage of one sword and one spear, they have given it quickly and generously to help send a mission team to build a church in rural Nicaragua, to make a down payment on a church lot in Manila, to underwrite a semester's study for a student preparing for Christian service in the inner city, or to bail out a young person in trouble. If they thought about it, the money would still be drawing 5 percent in the vaults of the bank.

Again, one man with little formal education knew that the company was taking advantage of its employees who were underpaid and worked under poor conditions. He went directly to the owner of the company and confronted him with the Christian principle of brotherhood and honesty. If he had waited for a more appropriate day or had considered taking a course in English grammar in preparation for the encounter, the battle would never have been waged nor the victory made possible. The owner of the company recognized the truth of the unlettered man's words and dramatically changed the working conditions and improved the pay scale. Speed and courage made the difference.

Wally is a new Christian. He has the physical appearance of a man who looks like he could fell a tree with one blow of the axe or drink a gallon of hard liquor. He is a burly, rugged-looking fellow. He usually sits in the rear of the church and watches for men, much like himself, who come to church at his invitation. He meets these men in the garage, on the street, in the restaurant, and on the highways. He knows what they are battling, and he does not hesitate to talk to men about the saving and transforming power of Jesus Christ. Sometimes he gets overeager and asks a seminary president, "Do you know Christ can save you?" Many times he helps long-time Christians to find their way back into fellowship with the Lord and with the church. Race, ethnic background, or faith are no barriers. He believes he has something that others are looking for and he tells them quickly. That is his style.

Most of us warm up slowly to strangers and use the route of building a friendship over time. Not Wally. He is Jonathan. Both approaches have their strengths and effectiveness. In fact, we may use both approaches hand in hand. Wally walks down the aisle with these men at invitation time and says to the minister, "Pastor, here's another one for Christ. I won him from the bottle, from an evil life. You teach him the way of Christ."

Wally also confided in his pastor that he would give anything for a few years of schooling so he could "talk sophisticated" to lost men. He, like Jonathan, uses what he has and achieves amazing results. Schooling would probably slow down his effectiveness. He knows the hearts and minds of men and speaks like a pro out of the depth of his heart directly to them and gets results. He is not surprised at the results because he, like Jonathan, knows he is a son of the King and that the sword he carries is the Word of God.

A Friend Who Is Closer Than a Brother (I Samuel 20:1-42)

We know Jonathan best in the friendship pact he made with David (I Samuel 20:12-17). It was an unusual friendship, for it was made between two men who stood on unequal terms. Jonathan was the son of a king; David was the son of a poor shepherd. Jonathan had the security of the royal house; David was a wanderer and a fugitive from the palace. Jonathan had everything going for him; David faced a very uncertain future. These two men made a covenant of friendship.

Most of us stand closer to Zebedee's wife (Matthew 20:20-21) than we do to Jonathan. We want the best for our children or for ourselves. We cherish the seats of honor, the first place in life, and the highest tributes. We work for them sometimes; sometimes we scheme or misuse other people to get them. Second place or second rate is far from our thinking. To think of putting someone else first is most difficult indeed. In fact, if someone else gets there, we say such things as, "You must be living right!" or "You lucky person!" We mourn easily with those who mourn, and we sorrow with those who suffer loss of material things or position in life. But to rejoice with one who outstripped us in the contest, or who was appointed to the position we wanted, is just not our cup of tea. Polite congratulations and notes of best wishes usually come when we realize that someone has to win and someone has to lose, and we don't want to be poor losers. But actually to help the other person get ahead of us is almost unthinkable.

Jonathan did this very thing! That is what made him an unusual man. In Philippians 2:3-4, Paul encouraged the Philippian Christians to look upon others as better than themselves and to see in their works greater deeds than their own. He said this was the way of Christ demonstrated in his self-sacrifice in the best interests of mankind.

Jonathan saw in David some real potential, and he wanted to be a part of David's future even though it meant second place for Jonathan. Someone has said that one can get an awful lot done if one doesn't care who gets the credit! Someone needs to say that one can get an awful lot done if one is willing to help someone else get it done.

Cleon Jones played right field for the New York Mets. Joe Christopher was also on the team. Joe was the regular, and Cleon played when Joe was out of the lineup. Joe saw something in Cleon and worked with him so much that Cleon got the right field position and Joe went to the bench. Eventually Joe was traded to a California team. One day, while waiting for the rain to let up, Joe was watching the game of the week. The Mets were playing. Cleon had been in a slump. Joe saw what was wrong, went to a pay phone, and called the Met's dugout and made a suggestion. Cleon tried it, got a hit, and broke the slump. Joe Christopher knows what Jonathan felt when he helped David to become a leader in Israel's political history.

The kind of living demonstrated in Jonathan's spirit takes a great deal of courage. An evangelistic life style may lead one to speak spontaneously to a perfect stranger like Wally does. Do it and you will win great victories for Christ and the church. It may lead one to give generously to help someone realize greater things than you or I have ever realized. Give and the kingdom will be enriched by a modern Jonathan.

A pastor can share the pulpit and parish duties with a young life and help prepare another Wesley or Moody. A church school teacher can share the class teaching and help prepare a great soul winner for years to come. An experienced deacon can coach a new Christian who can become a bigger and better influence in the community than the deacon ever dreamed possible. A teacher can encourage a student to exceed the highest prominence any teacher ever dreamed about. Churches, church schools, and Christians can not only call men and women to a saving knowledge of Jesus Christ, but also they can help men and women, boys and girls to realize their potential—even when they surpass us in our goals and dreams.

Jonathan knew what the evangelistic life style is meant to do—win and develop persons without envy or jealousy of spirit.

SHARING OUR INSIGHTS

The story of Jonathan is clearly a story about a style of life. We cannot read Fred Young's treatment of Jonathan without asking questions about our own behavior and style of life. How we make decisions and act upon them, how we witness to others, and how we feel about position and power are all life style questions that might be part of our reflection on this chapter.

1. "One man"—Fred Young declares that "one man . . . can start almost anything!" Do you really believe that? What did Jonathan do? Why was he effective? Was he really one man alone? In what ways could you be a Jonathan and get something started? What does it mean to act with integrity as one person in a position where decisions are made?

2. "Second place"—Jonathan was willing to take second place so that David, a person of more ability, could become king. Can you think of persons you know or have heard of who have done something similar? How do you feel when you see someone else in first place? Fred Young talks about an evangelistic life style being one in which we help people achieve their potential—help them grow. What are the ways in which your church helps people grow? What can you do to help people grow? What does helping people grow have to do with integrity?

3. "Both approaches hand in hand"—Fred Young uses Wally to illustrate the approach of a modern Jonathan to evangelism and compares him with the slower, more "sophisticated" way some of us might go about it. Do you find both approaches appropriate? With which are you most comfortable? Why? Are you able to identify with Jonathan as a model for evangelism? If both approaches go "hand in hand," how do you see them relating to each other? What does it mean to have integrity in the way you witness to another person?

4. "Readiness to move"—Fred Young stresses the fact that

Jonathan did not wait until everything was just right before moving. When is it appropriate to spend time planning, and when is it time to act? What is the relation between planning and action? Are there things you have been putting off until the right time? Are they things that you should be doing now? What does it mean to act decisively for God? What does being a person of integrity have to do with being ready to move?

Santiago Soto-Fontanez's style not only catches our attention, but it also makes Barnabas seem like one of our contemporaries and gives us insights about him that might otherwise be overlooked. Others are more well known, but they might *not* have been known if it were not for the ministry and encouragement of Barnabas. This wide-ranging interpretation of Barnabas shows an evangelistic life style which reaches into the whole of life: from economics to friendship, from disagreements in the church to divisions in society. Barnabas is seen as the first "true liberal" in the Christian movement.

Preparatory Reading: Acts 4:32-37; 9:22-29a; 11:19-26; 15:1-41.

Barnabas, the Man Who Encouraged Others
by Santiago Soto-Fontanez

His name was Joseph. Nobody ever called him Joe, for he had a presence and a dignity which were both attractive and awe-inspiring to those who met him for the first time. If you have seen a picture of the bust of Jupiter or Zeus, which is in the Vatican Museum of Rome, you may have an idea of how Joseph looked: the intelligent face, the piercing eyes, and the serene confidence are there. If a film were made about him, somebody like Charlton Heston would have to play the part. Once in a city called Lystra, in Asia Minor, this Joseph was mistaken for Jupiter, and some people even tried to worship him (Acts 14:12-13).

We first meet him in Jerusalem when the early church was beginning (Acts 4:36). Luke, the author of the book of Acts, describes him as a Levite, from Cyprus. Jews had been world travelers and merchants, and groups of them were to be found in almost all the great cities of the Roman Empire. Joseph's family had settled on the Greek island of Cyprus, but as was the custom, they kept their Jewish faith. So he was the heir of two cultures: Greek from the place of his birth and Jewish from his heritage from the priestly tribe of Israel. As you can see, his religious bent was not acquired: it was in his blood.

He may have come to Jerusalem as a young man, at the time another young man was preaching up and down the country. The New Testament does not tell us whether he knew Jesus personally, but Tertullian and others say that he was one of the seventy, that group of trainees who were sent by Jesus into the towns and villages to proclaim the gospel (Luke 10:1-2). If this was so, it is possible that he was also among the 120 in the upper room and so participated in the very start of the church.

Besides, he had a relative called Mary who owned a house in Jerusalem, a house which served as a gathering place of the first believers (Acts 12:12; Colossians 4:10). Some scholars even think that it was in the upper room of this same house where Jesus and his disciples had their last supper. Later that evening, when they left to go to Gethsemane to pray, the young son of this woman, curious and eager to know what was going on, followed the group into the Garden with a sheet as his only cover. When he found himself surrounded by police officers, he streaked home in the nude. Years later, he wrote about this incident which only he knew and could never forget (Mark 14:51-52).

There is no doubt that Joseph was very involved with the movement or the Way, as it was then called. He was a prominent figure in it. The early church was like our congregations or, for that matter, like any other group of society. People notice the personal characteristics and quirks of those who are in the forefront. They immediately dub them with usually appropriate descriptions. One may be the Critic, another Big Wind or Loud Mouth; another may be the Pessimist; and these descriptions usually fit.

The brethren in the early church had a name for Joseph. They called him Son of Consolation—or better translated, "Son of Encouragement." This really means "The Encourager," one who supports, inspires, and gives confidence to others. How and why they called him so we will discover as we follow his life in the New Testament, but the original adjective became part of his name used even more than his given name of Joseph. He was, from then on, Barnabas—"the Encourager." It was not a title; it was a description of a personality, the acknowledgment of character traits that were evident to everyone who came to know him. We may imagine him among the members of the early church, speaking to a young man who had just been converted, consoling the widow who had lost her husband, or helping a newcomer to Jerusalem get his bearings.

The fact that he was both Jew and Greek made him very useful in some situations. When the gospel was first preached to the Greeks who lived in Phoenicia and Antioch (Syria), and as many Gentiles believed, someone was needed to confirm them in their faith. The church in Jerusalem sent Barnabas (Acts 11:22-24) to Antioch for this purpose. And he did a good job because "a large company was added to the Lord." It is in this connection that we find another apt description of the Encourager: "he was a good man, full of the Holy Spirit and of faith" (Acts 11:24).

There is one small detail that may have escaped us before. As the result of this man's work in Antioch, "the disciples were for the first time called Christians" (Acts 11:26). Somehow, this Joseph Barnabas presented Christ so vividly, so earnestly, and with such insistence that he became "Mr. Christian," and with him all of those who have later believed in Christ have borne this name. A new life style had come into being, and those living it were marked forever. The name is a serious responsibility which every one of us carries to this day.

The Encourager and Social and Economic Responsibility (Acts 4:32-37)

"Deeds, not words, are what we need." We have heard this again and again because many people are most free with advice and instruction, but when it comes to the nitty-gritty, when the demand is for personal sacrifice, they just balk and give all kinds of excuses.

The early church gathered people from many backgrounds and economic conditions. There were among them, to be sure, people of means, but anybody who knows the Middle East must realize that countries in that part of the world have been poor, very poor indeed. Even today, with all the oil riches in the hands of their rulers, the masses live in wretched poverty. It was no different in the first century, and you can read in the New Testament how many offerings were sent to Jerusalem from the Gentile churches in Asia and Europe.

But we read an interesting statement about the early church: "There was not a needy person among them . . ." (Acts 4:34). The reason for this is clear. Living in the faith produced a sense of community and responsibility. Those who had possessions were happy to share with others everything they had. This was a new thing in the history of human relations. Here was a group of people who felt responsible one for the other, who made the welfare of their fellowmen a top concern. Some people have argued that the early church was communistic in organization, but they misread history. Their life together was not a political system but a very personal expression of their unity in Christ. Their concern for others was not imposed. It was voluntary; it was motivated by love and not by force. It was self-giving in the name of him who gave so much.

It should be noted that the early church was not a property-holding company. It was rather a distribution agency—a channel through which human needs were met. When a church in Pennsylvania mortgaged its property so as to make money available for the needs of the community, it was partly following the example of the early church. But how many congregations are willing to go that far?

It is in this setting that we first find Joseph Barnabas's name in the New Testament. He owned a field, and he sold it and brought the proceeds to the apostles for the common fund. If we accept the premise that every account found in the Scripture is put there for a purpose, there must be in Barnabas's action a greater meaning than we usually assign to the record. Was it to establish a contrast between a completely selfless action on the part of Barnabas and the dishonest and selfish conduct of Ananias and his wife?

Mr. Christian, the Encourager, set an example of social and economic responsibility for church leaders and for every Christian. At a time when the personal philosophy of so many is "What is in it for me?", we have to go back to the Scriptures and decide what his life tells us today.

True leaders must lead as much by their example as with their work. Barnabas was a real leader. He had made a commitment to a new way, a new life style, and that commitment required sacrifice, both of self and possessions. Barnabas lived up to his name. How better could he encourage other Christians to become "a serving community" than by coming forward and setting an example of total dedication?

We all know about persons today who have done just that. There was a lot of talk in the official board meeting of one church, but nobody knew what to do about the matter. A letter had been received from an inmate in the nearby state penitentiary. It said that, though he was up for parole and he hoped to be granted it, he might not be freed because he did not have an apartment or a job when he came out. There were some small businessmen on the board, but none of them had anything to offer. The wealthiest church member was of the opinion that this was a very delicate matter which should not be pushed.

Tom Brown heard all the arguments and opinions. When it seemed that these had been exhausted, he spoke in his usual soft and quiet way. He said, "I have been thinking about our church's responsibility toward these men. We as a church have failed to do our Christian duty when they have been in jail, and now we should do something. I own a house on Center Street which I shall make available to the church. Let us use it as a halfway house, to provide housing for men who are freed or paroled. Maybe some of our board members can offer them temporary employment, and this will help these men find their way again into society."

Tom Brown is not the richest of the members of the congregation, but he is an encourager, with a sense of social and economic responsibility. His action has helped persons without hope to find a new beginning in life. He is an example of an evangelistic life style in action.

The Encourager Shows Faith in Persons (Acts 9:27-29*a*; 11:25-26)

We like to speculate about things happening differently than they did. What if Andrew had not brought his brother to Jesus? How different would the history of the church have been without Simon Peter? What if the early believers had absolutely refused to accept into their fellowship the man who had persecuted them and probably caused some to die? They could have done it, you know!

This man Saul had been nothing but trouble for the early church. He had gone out of his way to torment, hound, and put in jail the believers, and his name must have brought fear and uneasiness to the members of the church. Suddenly he appeared in Jerusalem trying to join the fellowship and be received as a brother. We cannot blame the disciples for being afraid and suspicious. How can you trust a man like that? What if his conversion was faked and his baptism just a way of becoming a spy within the Movement in order to wreck it? It is so difficult to have faith in persons, especially if they have a record such as this man had.

"But Barnabas took him, and brought him to the apostles . . ." (Acts 9:27). Barnabas took upon himself the task of introducing Saul to the apostles, and he succeeded. The Christian church owes a huge debt to the Encourager for helping Saul enter the company of the early church. Barnabas showed, in the new life style which he lived, that faith in persons was a needed and valuable factor.

This is why Barnabas is such an outstanding personality. F. J. Foakes Jackson describes him thus:

> Barnabas indeed is one of the most attractive characters in the New Testament. He possessed the rare gift of discerning merit in others. Probably inferior in ability to Paul, he was his superior in Christian graces. He seems to have been utterly without jealousy, eager to excuse the faults of others, quick to recognize merit, ready to compromise for the sake of peace. Paul's elevation of character makes him scarcely human, whilst the virtues of Barnabas make him singularly lovable. The Paul of history contributes to the progress of the world, Barnabas and those like him make it endurable to live in it. Whilst we admit the greatness of Paul, we cannot forget that Barnabas was the real pioneer of a world-embracing Christianity.[1]

The other night I was watching a talk program on television. One of the guests, a well-known star in show business, turned to the M.C. and said: "You may have forgotten, but you gave me my first chance in this business. I was a young fellow, unknown and scared. It seemed nobody wanted me. You had a program in such and such a station and you used me, and that was my first real chance. After that, I got offers from many others."

It is very easy to forget the beginnings of our success and especially the people who helped us take the first steps. As you read the report on Paul's life, which he put in the first chapter of the letter to the Galatians, you notice that some important details are missing (Galatians 1:12, 14). He has forgotten how he came to be accepted by the apostles (Acts 9:26-29a), and he does not mention the fact that Barnabas went all the way to Tarsus to bring him to Antioch (Acts 11:25-26). This was Saul's great chance. It was Antioch from which he started his world mission.

Encouragers have to realize that human memory is weak, and gratitude is not too common even among men of God—that attempts to reconcile differences among persons may be judged as weaknesses

---

[1] F. J. Foakes Jackson, *The Acts of the Apostles,* The Moffatt New Testament Commentary (New York: Harper & Row, Publishers, 1931), p. 100, quoted in *The Interpreter's Bible* (Nashville: Abingdon Press, 1954), vol. 9, p. 149.

and even treason. Barnabas could put up with all these things, because he was "a good man, full of the Holy Spirit and of faith." So was Paul, too, but their ministries would eventually take different directions, and Paul would become the star. Yet Barnabas, the Encourager, is still greatly needed. We may find some like him even among us, in our churches.

A young fellow started to come to a church. Though he was dressed properly and behaved in a quiet way, there was something about him which people found disturbing. He had a colorless complexion; his eyes were sunken and reddish; and when you looked at him, he would not meet your eyes.

Somebody recognized him and whispered in a neighbor's ear: "He is a drug addict. . . . He is related to So and So, but he has been on drugs." From one person to the other, the word went very rapidly. At the end of the service many "good people" avoided him as he stood to one side. They did not tell him he was not welcome there; they did not have to.

Frank Smith, a young member of the board of deacons, approached the visitor. He talked to him, and they left the church together to have a cup of coffee at a nearby luncheonette. The young man, whom we will call Pete, told Frank his story. His parents were respectable, middle-class Christians, and as a child he had attended Sunday school. He started experimenting with drugs while in high school, went on to college, and became hooked on the stuff. His family relations had become at first strained and then completely broken. He had quit college and had gone from job to job, sometimes trying to get rid of the monkey on his back, other times giving in without a fight.

Recently Pete had, by chance, attended a meeting of young Christian people. Somebody had told him that it was another kind of group. There he heard that Jesus Christ could free him from the modern devil of drug addiction, and he decided then and there to find out whether this was true. He prayed to God and decided to quit drugs "cold turkey," that is to say, not gradually but immediately. For days he suffered great agony, but with his newborn faith he was able to resist going back. Now he was looking for a support group, a fellowship which could help him hold fast to his decision. But in that particular church he felt that people distrusted him and were avoiding him. He might not return to its services.

Frank talked to him as a friend. No judgment about Pete's past life was expressed, and no self-righteous attitude was shown. "I want you to continue coming to our services. I will sit with you and will introduce you to other members." Frank did just that. Several months later Pete was asked to speak to the young people's group about his experience. Others started to talk to him, and today Pete has gone back to college and is a lay preacher, speaking out of his own experience about the saving power of the gospel. He wants to be a Christian minister.

Frank Smith is a modern encourager; through his faith in people, he, like Barnabas, befriended one shunned by others, one who was suspected and avoided by the "good" members of the church. Pete may still become a Christian minister because somebody had enough faith in God's power to renew life.

Through our whole nation there are people looking for a supporting community. Christians who understand the evangelistic life style will open their fellowship to these people and will reinforce their faith and strengthen their lives.

The Encourager Believes in a Second Chance (Acts 15:36-41)

John Mark was a city boy. He came from a well-to-do family and moved freely among the founders of the early church. He was Barnabas's cousin (Colossians 4:10) and went with him to Antioch when Barnabas was sent to confirm the faith of the Gentile believers there.

When the church in Antioch decided to send the first missionaries to the Gentile world (Acts 13:1-3), Barnabas and Saul were commissioned. It is evident, from a later passage, that they took with them the young man John Mark. The trip took them to Cyprus, the native island of Barnabas, and there some exciting things happened. Then the missionaries decided to go to the mainland of Asia Minor to continue their work (Acts, chapters 13, 14). As the work started in Asia, however, John Mark left the two older men and returned home (Acts 13:13).

Several reasons have been suggested for Mark's apparent desertion. Was he afraid of the hardships of the missionary campaign? Was the increasing authority of Paul resented by Mark as he saw his cousin being put in a secondary role by the more aggressive man? Did he see his commitment only covering the trip to Cyprus and not farther? The record only tells us that Mark left and returned home (Acts 13:13).

A year or more went by. Paul and Barnabas came back from their missionary journey, gave their report, and went to Jerusalem to defend the interests of the Gentile believers (Acts 15). Back in Antioch, they started to plan another campaign. When it came to decide whom they were to take as assistants, there was trouble between the missionaries. It seems that Mark was back in Antioch and Barnabas wanted to take him along. Paul did not want to hear about it. "How can we take a man who deserted us? No excuses! He is no good; he does not have it! I do not want him around!" So it went, with Barnabas arguing in his defense and, at last, both men losing their tempers and breaking their team. Barnabas left with John Mark for Cyprus, while Paul took Silas and went the other way into Asia. It is even thought that while Paul and Silas were sent with the church's blessing (Acts 15:40), Barnabas and Mark did not get its support.

While tradition tells us quite a bit about Barnabas, little more is told about him in the New Testament after this incident. We know that he continued his missionary labors with no financial support (I Corinthians 9:6) and that he and Paul reestablished a friendly relationship, as evidenced by Paul's reference to Mark in 2 Timothy 4:11. But Paul came to be the star and became known as the "Apostle to the Gentiles."

We know more about the young man who caused all the trouble. As a writer, Mark gave us the one document which served the other authors of the later Gospels as a source of information on the life of Jesus. In the first three centuries of the church, Mark was known as the "interpreter of Peter," a phrase which has been accepted to mean that he wrote mostly from the point of view of Peter's interpretation of the gospel.

Barnabas evidently believed in giving a person a second chance, and he was not mistaken in having insisted on retaining Mark. As the Encourager, Barnabas could not accept that a man should be declared a failure because of a mistake or a momentary weakness. In defending Mark, he was not doing it because of his kinship to him, but because he was aware of ability and possibilities which others may have not seen.

People who understand the evangelistic life style have to believe in a second chance and even in a third and fourth. God gives us not one chance but many chances to make good. The Bible is full of accounts of the lives of men whom God used, even after successive failures.

Jack was a bright young fellow, though full of mischief. He had decided on the ministry while in his second year of college, during a Spiritual Emphasis week at the school. He went on to finish his B.A. with good grades and started his seminary training the following fall.

After the freewheeling life in college, life in the seminary was a little boring. Jack enlivened it with a few foolish pranks. One night, with another student, he broke into the closed pantry and got some food, which they offered to some of the other students. Naturally, somebody told who the culprits were. Both students were called by the dean and had to come before a committee of the faculty. The case was open and shut. A break-in had occurred and goods had been stolen. The students had confessed. They had to be punished, and the usual sentence was to be thrown out of school. The young men were sent out of the room while the faculty voted on the case.

Professor Truehart interrupted the proceedings. He asked in his mild way, "Should we not give these boys another chance?" Professor Stronglaw argued heatedly that this could not be. That kind of permissiveness was the cause of the moral state of the nation. A crime had been committed and only by punishing the culprits as harshly as possible could they be straightened out. Some of the other teachers agreed. But Professor Truehart insisted: "Will expelling them really change them? Why not put them on probation and try to help them with Christian understanding?" Back and forth, the arguments continued, but luckily a majority of the faculty committee was moved by Dr. Truehart's counsel. Jack's career was saved, and he continued his seminary training and graduated.

Today Jack has been a successful pastor for a number of years and is known as an able denominational leader. An encourager saved an otherwise lost career and kept a good man in the ministry.

The Encourager—a True Christian Liberal (Acts 11:19-26; Acts 13:46)

In our day, the word "liberal" has lost its real meaning and has taken on many negative ones. People often assign to a so-called liberal all kinds of antisocial and immoral ideas which have little to do with true liberal thinking, motives, and actions. Religiously speaking, a liberal is frequently judged by the beliefs he does not accept or the things he denies rather than by what he stands for and those beliefs he positively holds.

The true liberal as one "not narrow in mind, not bound by authoritarianism, orthodoxy, or traditional or established forms in action, attitude, or opinion" *(Webster's Third New International Dictionary)* is a progressive person who will adopt innovations when these help other human beings achieve their full development. According to this definition, Joseph Barnabas, the Encourager, was the first liberal of the Christian movement.

Barnabas appears in the roster of the primitive church as a man whose main concern was people—not people in general, but persons. This preoccupation with individuals moved him to adopt a liberal stance and defend it. The fact that those whom he encouraged became more important than he himself speaks for the character of the man and of his personal philosophy.

Out of his liberal stance he contributed to the process by which the Christian faith broke out of its Jewish origins and became a doctrine of salvation for all persons. For many of the early disciples of Christ who were Jewish, the kingdom of God was their kingdom (Acts 1:6); the Messiah was their messiah; salvation had to be their particular salvation and nobody else's. What Jesus had said about the universal fatherhood of God and the instructions he gave about going into all the world were either misunderstood or ignored. Even Peter, who in a miraculous way had been sent to a Gentile home (Acts 10) and had given a report of his visit, went back to his nationalistic and biased position (Galatians 2:11-12).

The early Christian community was afraid of the church losing its Jewish character, and there was a long struggle to prevent it. But it had to happen, and the change would come only when somebody dared to break with tradition and confront the establishment in a creative way.

Barnabas was, according to some scholars, the real pioneer of work among the Gentiles. Nobody can measure the impact of his ideas on Paul nor can we prove that it was Barnabas's influence which turned Paul toward a world perspective on Christianity and its relationship to the Gentiles. But in the beginning, as the church started work among the non-Jews, Barnabas's name is the first mentioned, Paul's being second (Acts 13:1-2; 15:12). We find the liberal Christian doing a two-way job for the early church, the importance of which we sometimes overlook.

Barnabas served as the apostles' representative to the Gentile converts (Acts 11:19-26). As a result of the persecution which arose over Stephen, many Christians from Jerusalem fled to other cities, some even out of the country into Phoenicia and Syria. But they spoke at first "to none except Jews," which was very much in accordance with their idea that Jesus' message was for them. Among these Jews were some born in Cyprus and North Africa. They did speak to the Greeks in Antioch. To their surprise, the Gentiles also believed, in great numbers.

The news of this development reached Jerusalem, and for some this must have been disturbing, if not unwelcome, news. The church decided to send the Encourager to Antioch. It says in the Scripture (Acts 11:23) that he was glad when he saw the working of the grace of God. So he told the new converts to keep the faith. But he did more.

He remembered Saul, who was in his hometown of Tarsus. He decided that this was the spot for a man of Saul's background and education. "So Barnabas went to Tarsus to look for Saul; and when he had found him, he brought him to Antioch" (verses 25-26). There they stayed for over a year. When a great famine came and the brethren in Jerusalem were suffering, Barnabas and Saul carried relief to those in Judea.

Again, we may ask ourselves what would have happened if, instead of an open-minded, liberal believer, somebody else had gone to the new Gentile converts and started (as some later did) to insist that they had no right to be Christians—not being Jews—and that they should cease and desist. God used Barnabas to bring assurance to these people, the very first people ever called Christians!

We have already mentioned the commissioning of the first missionaries to the Gentile world, their first journey, and their return to Antioch. Their report was a joyous one, as they told "all that God had done with them, and how he had opened a door of faith to the Gentiles" (Acts 14:27). They stayed for a prolonged time with the church in Antioch.

A real crisis developed when men from Judea came to Antioch and started teaching the need for the Gentiles to become Jews before they could be Christians. There was dissension and debate, and finally the matter was referred to the church in Jerusalem. A council was called, and Barnabas and Paul, who had been appointed by the church in Antioch, went to Jerusalem. There they would plead the cause of the Gentile Christians against the demands of believers who belonged to the party of the Pharisees (Acts 15:5).

Peter spoke first and his attitude was favorable to the new converts. Then Barnabas and Paul related what God had done through them among the Gentiles. The arguments were finished, and a compromise was worked out by which the Gentiles were freed from most of the rituals but were asked to keep the ethical principles of the Jewish faith.

The really important thing was the acknowledgment of the principle that conformity to a culture was not essential to becoming a follower of Jesus. There was room for persons of different backgrounds and forms of worship, as long as the basic unity of belief was kept intact. That was the turning point of the Christian church. Barnabas played a big part in bringing this about. He was a true liberal spirit, sensitive to the feelings of others and much aware of the life situation of those outside the Jewish faith, who had come to accept Jesus.

As we try to live the evangelistic life style in our time, Barnabas is set as an example of what this really means. His spirit of sacrifice, his faith in people, his willingness to give a second chance to others, and his open-mindedness, understanding, and tolerance are needed today as much as ever in our personal relationships, in our group life, and in our effort to influence institutions. "For he was a good man, full of the Holy Spirit and of faith . . . and in Antioch the disciples were for the first time called Christians" (Acts 11:24, 26*b*).

SHARING OUR INSIGHTS

The richness and humanity of Barnabas, as portrayed by Santiago Soto-Fontanez, make him an appealing person from whom we can learn much. His life style reflects a radical commitment; yet it is expressed so naturally and easily and lovingly that it hardly seems unusual. Both the simple humanity of the man and his radical commitment suggest several areas for possible further discussion.

1. "Encourager"—Barnabas's name underlines his role as an encourager. In what ways is Barnabas an encourager? What persons have been "Barnabas" to you in your life? In what ways are you an encourager? In what ways could you become an encourager? Who are the people you know who need encouragement? What does being an encourager have to do with integrity?

2. "Gratitude not common"—some of those whom Barnabas encouraged became far more well known than he. Are there times when we have forgotten to thank those who encouraged

us? Have you ever helped someone along the way to a greater ministry? You never know whom you are going to influence in what ways. The story of Barnabas suggests that even the simplest of your relationships with another person may have significance for the whole world. Reflect on your daily routine. What persons do you meet each day? What roles do you play—mother, father, friend, church school teacher, boss, employee? How can you be a Barnabas in some of those relationships? What does it mean to have integrity when helping someone else grow?

3. "A distribution agency"—the Scripture says "they had everything in common." Barnabas sold some of his property and gave it to this early Christian community. The church was the point at which the necessities of life got redistributed so that no one remained in need. Does this description fit the church as you know it? What would a church today look like if it followed this model? What would it mean for you to take seriously Barnabas's example in this act? What does it mean to have integrity in relation to property, wealth, and those in need? What does it mean for the church to be a "distribution agency"?

4. "Conformity to a certain culture"—along with some of the other studies in this series, the story of Barnabas reminds us that being Christian is something different than accepting the standards of behavior of a particular nation. Gentiles did not have to adopt Jewish behavior to become Christian. Are there things that we expect of new Christians that are more a matter of American or community custom than central to the faith? What are the requirements for membership in your church? Do all members agree on the same requirements? Are the requirements in your church the same as in other churches you know? In what ways does the story of Barnabas help you resolve such questions? What does it mean to treat new Christians with integrity in terms of what is expected of them?

5. "Second chance"—Santiago Soto-Fontanez uses Barnabas's attitude toward Mark to stress the importance, in an evangelistic life style, of giving people another chance. Has anyone ever given you a second chance? Do you know people who have been given a second chance and, like Jack, have gone on to make something of their lives? Do you know someone now who needs a second chance? What does integrity have to do with giving people a second chance? Why should anyone get a second chance? Have you more frequently been like Paul or like

Barnabas in your attitude toward people who showed weakness? In what kinds of situations do you find it hard to give persons a second chance? Would people like Pete, in this study, get a "second chance" in your church?

6. "Liberal"—Santiago Soto-Fontanez calls Barnabas the first true liberal in the Christian movement. How do you feel about that interpretation? What comes to your mind when you hear the word "liberal" applied to a Christian? Is that what Dr. Soto-Fontanez means? What kind of liberal was Barnabas? Do you find yourself able to identify with Barnabas as a liberal? What does integrity have to do with being liberal?

III. SOME EVANGELISTIC LIFE STYLE CONCLUSIONS

by Owen D. Owens in collaboration with R. James Ogden

INTRODUCTION

Seven times we have looked at a biblical person and compared our experiences with his or hers. Each biblical person has been different, and at the same time, all of them have had some things in common. Each of us has identified with some of them more than with others. We have been challenged more by some than by others. Our reactions have been as varied as the personalities we have studied and as different as we ourselves are as people. Chances are, however, that each of us has learned something from every study.

To this point, attention has been focused mainly on each biblical person in isolation. This section seeks to look at all of them together. It is time to try summarizing what we have learned. Owen Owens will share with you some of the things that have happened to him as he worked through each of these studies. He will ask some questions and suggest some directions for your thought. His report of his experience may stimulate your own thinking. But the basic work of this session is for you to reach some of your own conclusions about the meaning of an evangelistic life style and being a person of integrity.

A SUMMARY OF ONE PERSON'S RESPONSE

Parts of this section will be written in the first person because they are my statements of what happened to me, Owen Owens, as I worked with these Bible studies. The "Sharing Our Insights" section at the end of the chapter suggests a way in which every reader might go through the same process to clarify his or her conclusions. The impact of these studies will be realized only as each person becomes a part of the continuing journey of faith, putting into his or her own words and behavior what it means to respond to God.

103

The Impact of Each Biblical Person

As a way of reviewing the seven biblical persons, I have asked myself four questions:

1. What one word would I use to summarize what I saw going on in this story?
2. What one thing did I learn from this story about integrity?
3. In what one way does this story challenge me to change?
4. What one insight did I gain from this story about the meaning of an evangelistic life style?

I deliberately did not attempt to identify the main point in the story nor did I try to summarize the writer's thinking. This is a personal report of what "grabbed" me. The truth in each of these stories will work itself out differently in the life of each reader.

Nicodemus

One word that summarizes: Power. Being born from above means seeing God's power expressed in acts of self-giving love for others.
One thing about integrity: Wholeness, or integrity, means being able to use influence for good, and not for evil. We see extraordinary displays of power today. Think of rockets which go to the moon and of atomic bombs, or think of huge businesses whose smallest decisions affect the lives of millions. Tragically, we modern people seem no more able to use our vast powers for good than were the people of Jesus' time able to do. Even worse, just like Nicodemus, all of this power confuses us about God. Jesus tells us, therefore, to look for God in a man lifted up from the earth on a cross. As he pointed out to Nicodemus, God is the One who uses influence for good, loving the world so much that he gave his only Son.
One way I am challenged: I may not have much influence, but my life touches my wife, children, people at work, and many others. In my gardening, fishing, and consuming, I also touch the land. I feel challenged to come further into the light, so that I use my influence for good, and not for evil.
One insight about an evangelistic life style: An evangelistic life style begins and ends with the gospel of Jesus Christ, nowhere more sharply stated than in John 3:16. Such a self-giving love leads disciples, as it did Jesus, toward a style of life in which power and influence are used for good and not evil.

Job

One word that summarizes: Suffering. Job has lost his prosperity, family, health, standing in the community, and even God. Alone, he takes his case before God.

One thing about integrity: Job had withstood two threats to his integrity, prosperity, and suffering. He could not understand God. When the Lord spoke to Job, he repented in dust and ashes, and thus he *became* a person of integrity: ". . . he was . . . aware of the divine resource, and he could make it. So can we."

One way I am challenged: Job challenges me to believe in God, for if the Lord can truly speak out of the midst of the worst storms of life, then divine control is complete. Neither prosperity nor suffering can separate us from the Lord.

One insight about an evangelistic life style: Job has as much understanding of ecology as any book of the Bible. He knows human beings can mine precious metals, dam up the rivers, and even overturn mountains by the roots (28:9-11). He also knows that science and industrial technology are not the ways to wisdom. The fear of the Lord is wisdom, and to depart from evil is understanding (28:28). Good stewardship, so essential to an evangelistic life style, begins when we start to show some humility toward the creatures which God has created. After all, when we have drawn all the Leviathans from the deep and have exterminated the last of the great sperm whales, will we be ready to put something new in their place? Instead we are turning created order into chaos. Rather than seeking further "progress" through science and technology, departing from such evil is understanding.

Ruth

One word that summarizes: Risk. In this book, two women who have nothing "must risk bold, even shocking, acts for the sake of survival and the hope of the blessing."

One thing about integrity: Poor and downtrodden persons gain integrity by asserting themselves. The Lord has a special blessing for those of "low degree" (Luke 1:52), which he gives in this world. Ruth and Naomi lay hold of that promised blessing by being aggressively feminine, modeling for us a radical faith which dares to risk all.

One way I am challenged: As a white man, do I have the courage of a Boaz to support one who comes to me risking everything? Or will I go down in history as that nameless kinsman who acted only out of selfish interest?

One insight about an evangelistic life style: As in the time of Ruth, women today are asserting their rights as human beings. Some men will respond by using religion to protect their selfish interests, just as slave owners once quoted the Bible to "prove" that slavery was ordained by God. They forget that God does not want those of low degree to "stay in their place," but instead he lifts them up. An evangelistic life style follows the way of Ruth and Boaz, boldly taking risks and leaving the blessing to God.

Nehemiah

One word that summarizes: Rebuilding. When warfare or "benign neglect" lays waste land and city, God calls out builders to put things back together again.

One thing about integrity: Being a whole person means giving oneself for one's people. Nehemiah was successful, but he did not act to advance his own economic self-interest. Instead he risked losing his position and financial security by asking the king to be allowed to rebuild Jerusalem. A person of integrity, therefore, sees the ruins, has compassion, and uses one's energy to rebuild.

One way I am challenged: Very often I feel like the people of Jerusalem, who got tired and threatened and lost sight of the vision. Nehemiah encourages me to be obedient to the heavenly vision and to keep trying.

One insight about an evangelistic life style: We Americans have had little experience with rebuilding. The very first pioneers used up the land and then moved on to carve out new farms from the wilderness, where they repeated the process. As our cities have aged, we have abandoned them to the poor and have built suburbs and new towns on farmland. Now there are few frontiers left. We need an evangelistic life style which will call out rebuilders, such as Nehemiah, able to tackle a wasteland inhabited by despairing people and to create a new city out of the rubble.

Peter

One word that summarizes: Forthright. Peter was a direct man, almost brash. "What he felt, he expressed."

One thing about integrity: Fear is a very grave threat to being a whole person. The storm on the lake and the mob at the trial of Jesus were very real physical threats to Peter's life. The conflict between parties in the early church threatened his leadership. Seeking to save himself, in all three instances he denied what he stood for. The first two times Jesus intervened to give Peter a new start—the third time it appears to have been Paul who did so. But each time Peter repented and started over, he was a more whole person than previously.

One way I am challenged: Peter's forthrightness made it possible for him to live a life of discipleship fully, experiencing both the highs and the lows. He challenges me to be more open with others, knowing that when fear overcomes me and my integrity gets broken, God will reach out and lift me up.

One insight about an evangelistic life style: Peter's life shows me that the one essential of an evangelistic life style is persistent discipleship. The ongoing reality of God is so powerful that Peter could be forgiven even after denying Jesus three times. God had a mission for Peter—to feed his sheep. Peter made many mistakes, but he learned from them and was able to follow that mission to the end.

Jonathan

One word that summarizes: Loyalty. Jonathan loved David and remained loyal to him even when he saw that David, and not he, was going to be the next king.

One thing about integrity: The covenanted word of a person of integrity is good, even when it comes to putting someone else first. Thus David was able to depend on Jonathan to do what he said he would.

One way I am challenged: Jonathan challenges me to accept the gifts of others and to support those who can make greater contributions to the well-being of everyone than I.

One insight about an evangelistic life style: Being successful often means trying to cut others down so you can get ahead of them. Instead, an evangelistic life style is meant to "win and develop persons without envy or jealousy of spirit."

Barnabas

One word that summarizes: Encouragement. Barnabas was a person who gave courage to others, not only by recognizing God-given gifts and calling them out, but also by presenting Christ so vividly that he became "Mr. Christian."

One thing about integrity: Being a person of integrity who encourages others and calls forth their gifts does not always issue in gratitude, "even among men of God." Barnabas encouraged because this was his nature and calling, not for the rewards which might come. Wholeness is its own reward.

One way I am challenged: Barnabas challenges me to be more steadfast in my encouragement of others. Just as I have benefited from his work through being able to read the Gospel of Mark and the letters of Paul, perhaps someone in the future will benefit from my efforts.

One insight about an evangelistic life style: Interdependence is a central feature characterizing an evangelistic life style. Barnabas shows us how people become interdependent in Christ, as he brought Saul to the apostles, supported Mark when Paul would have thrown him out of missionary work, and argued the cause of the Gentiles at the Jerusalem Council.

Some Common Themes in the Stories of These Biblical Persons

Each person is unique. As we have seen, each story we have considered is different from the others. Some common themes, however, seem to appear in most of the stories.

1. Faith in God came primarily by hearing and believing the witness of the generations who had gone before. There is no evidence that God spoke directly to anyone other than Job. In fact, Jesus even turned Nicodemus's attention away from miraculous acts which supposedly would prove the divine reality, to the fact that God's power is revealed in self-giving love for others. We look for God in the wrong places. The Lord is revealed again and again in our experiences daily. Jonathan, Ruth, Nehemiah, and, above all, Barnabas show us what it means to believe in a God who loves the world, and to live out that belief in action.

2. Each biblical person was a decisive, aggressive actor, not a pawn. Not one was a victim of fate, passively allowing life to push her or him around. Job refused to curse God and die when he had lost everything which made life worth living. He took his case before the Almighty—and God honored him by speaking directly. (God also refused to let Job back out; "Gird up your

loins like a man," the Lord said.) Jonathan was not only a forceful military leader, but also he was one who refused to knuckle under to the pressure of his father, the king; he kept his word and maintained his integrity. Ruth and Naomi made brave and bold decisions in their struggle to survive and find new blessing. Peter said what he thought, acted decisively, and took the consequences. Nicodemus risked the disapproval of his religious group when he came to see Jesus. Nehemiah rebuilt Jerusalem, refusing to hide when enemies threatened or to give up when his own people let him down. Barnabas touched the lives of thousands through his missionary work, argued the Gentile case before the Jerusalem council, and challenged Paul to his face when he gave up on Mark.

Not one of our biblical persons used religion as an escape from the hard realities of this world. No, instead faith in God gave "courage to be." The Lord, furthermore, appears to honor persons who assert themselves. Each was blessed in appropriate ways in this life, and their stories are told and retold so that their names are not forgotten.

3. Biblical persons were surprisingly honest about themselves, as are the stories about them. Just as with God-inspired persons in our time, when we get close, we see warts as well as beauty. Peter collapsed under pressure; Job complained. Nehemiah was a proud autocrat (for instance, showing little sympathy for the families he broke up). Jonathan was too idealistic, as his father warned him (1 Samuel 20:31). Nicodemus was afraid of being seen associating with a controversial person. If we look closely, we see that Ruth, Barnabas, and Peter also were very human beings. Apparently being a person of integrity frees one from having to pretend one is better than one actually is.

4. Finally, encouragers are critically important. Persons like David, Ruth, or Paul may shape history, but without Jonathan, Boaz, and Barnabas, their efforts would have been futile. Encouragers reveal the kinds of self-giving love which create community where there was only hostility.

Evangelistic Life Style: A Concluding Summary

There are many things we have learned about an evangelistic life style. To begin with, we have seen that it deals with basic human concerns. Where do I (Nicodemus) see the divine power revealed? Since I (Job) am a person of integrity, why am I suffering? What risks should I (Ruth) take to survive and be blessed? Am I (Nehemiah) able to rebuild the city? How far should I (Jonathan) go in being loyal to my friend? Why am I (Peter) so forthright and direct—it always gets me into trouble? Should I (Barnabas) keep on encouraging others even when no one seems to appreciate me?

Second, we have seen that biblical persons learned about the reality and nature of God from those who went before them. Today many wonder whether there can be a God who is both good and in control of the world. We can refer such persons to the biblical conviction that faith in a good and powerful God is a matter of *faith*—i.e., hearing and believing the witness of those who had gone before them. The good news of God offers each the opportunity to be made whole and to have one's life make a positive impact on the world. Believing the gospel means seizing the opportunity, taking the risk that this way is true, and allowing the Lord to honor the Word in one's own experience. Jonathan, Ruth, Job, and Barnabas give us hope that we, too, may believe and find meaning, power, and opportunity.

Third, living out an evangelistic life style means being a decisive, aggressive actor, not a pawn. A whole person is not weak and ineffective, but a complete human being. Our frailties even serve as occasions to bring us closer to the Lord, thus enhancing our effectiveness (as with Job and Peter). The biblical persons we have studied, therefore, did not have to hide their sinful and fallible ways. Neither did they wallow in their weaknesses. Being a person of integrity means using one's gifts and fallibilities—one's whole self— to complete the mission set before one. For some it will be to escape from famine and poverty to find blessing and self-respect. For others it will be to seek God and meaning for life as a survivor of the holocaust. For still others it will be to rebuild ruined cities. Mission is unique to each member of the people of God. A harmonious church appears only when each of us lives a life to the full in expressions of self-giving love. If we are faithful, our life stories may someday give hope to those who follow us, even as have the lives of the persons recorded in the Bible.

SHARING OUR INSIGHTS

1. Look back over the biblical persons in this study series, and attempt to summarize what you have learned about each person, using the headings that were used in this chapter as guidelines:

    (1) What one word would I use to summarize what I saw going on in this story?

(2) What one thing did I learn from the story about integrity?

(3) In what way does this story challenge me to change?

(4) What one insight about the meaning of an evangelistic life style did I gain from this story?

2. List what you see to be some of the common themes in these stories of biblical persons.

3. Write a paragraph or two to express some of the final conclusions you have reached as a result of these studies, about an evangelistic life style and becoming a person of integrity, in terms of their meaning for you today. You might begin with the phrase, "For me an evangelistic life style is. . . ." One or more sentences might deal with "To be a person of integrity means. . . ."

4. Share some of your conclusions with the group, including some first action steps you intend to take as a result of this study.

5. Share in a decision as a group to undertake some particular action as a result of this shared study experience.